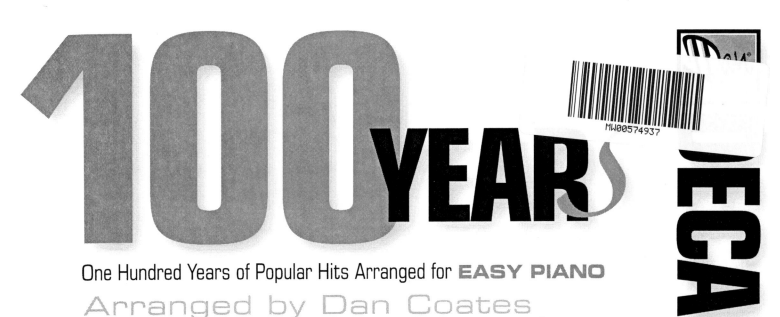

100 YEARS

One Hundred Years of Popular Hits Arranged for **EASY PIANO**

Arranged by Dan Coates

DECADE by DECADE

Anyone who plays the piano has experienced the joy of playing that certain song that lights up their audience and brings everybody together—whether it's a packed concert hall or a casual gathering of friends or relatives. Popular songs have the unique ability spark memories, as well as create new ones, and every generation has their favorites.

This handy and valuable volume equips pianists with a diverse array of songs that are guaranteed to delight any audience. The most universally beloved songs from an entire century of popular music are compiled here, from classic standards to smash hit singles and movie themes. These are the songs that every pianist should have in their repertoire.

The great sounding, easy-to-play arrangements in this folio are the work of internationally acclaimed piano arranger Dan Coates. Coates has the unique talent of coaxing lush, professional sounds out of arrangements that are surprisingly simple to master, even for the casual hobbyist. Fun facts about each each piece are included to broaden understanding of pop music history and to put all of these mega-hits into perspective. For practice, performance, or pleasure, the more than 250 pages of music in this book ensure unlimited hours of enjoyment for pianists and audiences of all ages.

Alfred

Produced by
Alfred Music
P.O. Box 10003
Van Nuys, CA 91410-0003
alfred.com

ISBN-10: 0-7390-8879-3
ISBN-13: 978-0-7390-8879-1

Contents

AQUARIUS

"Aquarius" originated in the 1969 musical *Hair*, a revolutionary work which defined the "rock musical" genre and ran for thousands of performances on Broadway and in London. The Fifth Dimension released a medley of "Aquarius" and "Let the Sunshine In" (one of the numbers from the second act) in 1969. It held the #1 position on the Billboard Hot 100 chart for six weeks and went platinum.

Music by Galt MacDermot
Words by James Rado and Gerome Ragni
Arranged by Dan Coates

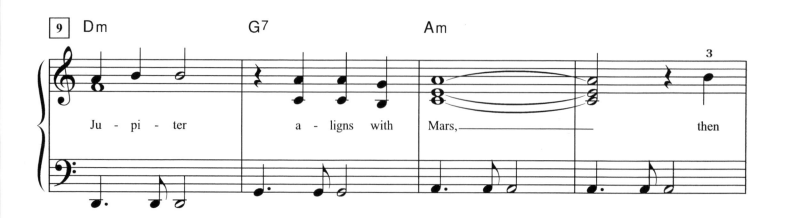

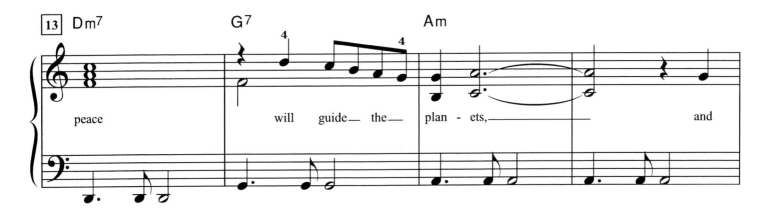

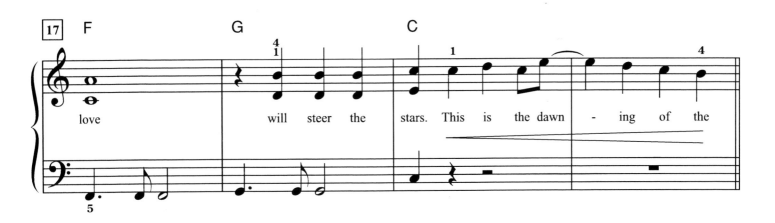

Chorus:

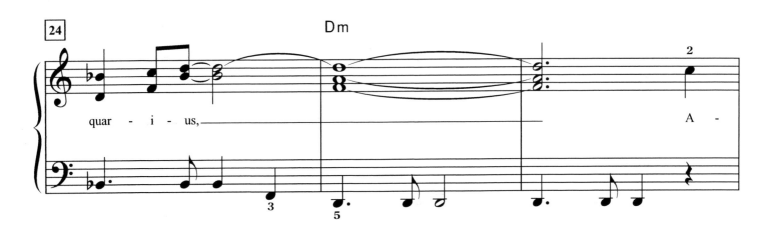

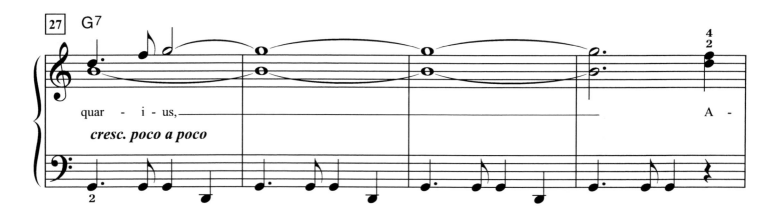

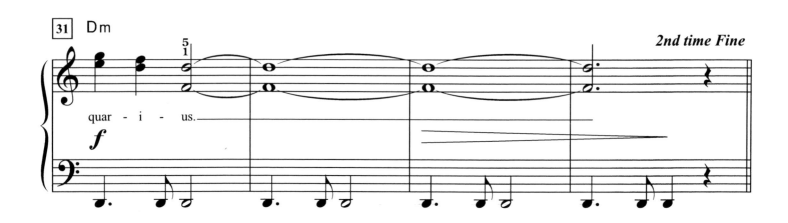

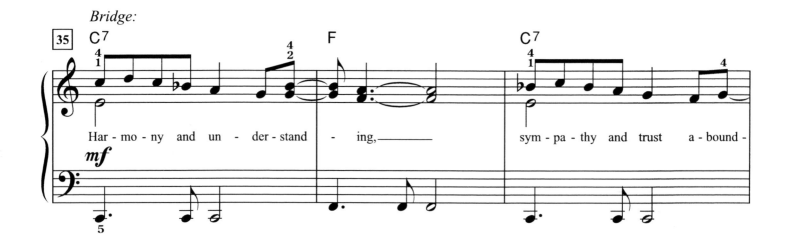

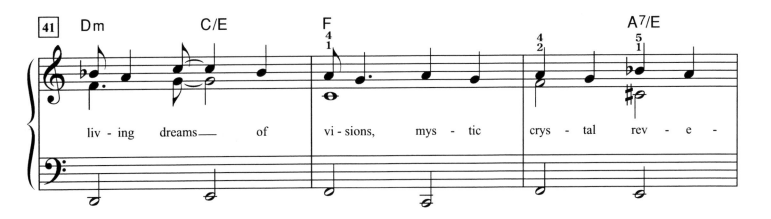

living dreams—— of vi - sions, mys - tic crys - tal rev - e -

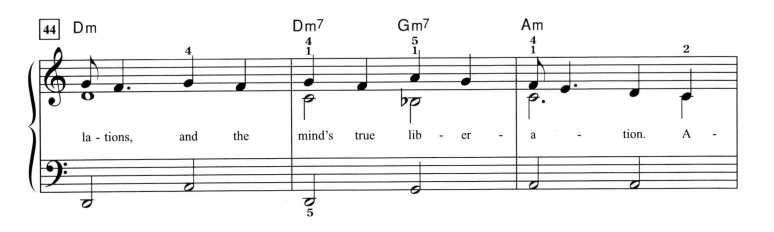

la - tions, and the mind's true lib - er - a - tion. A -

quar - i - us,—— A -

cresc.

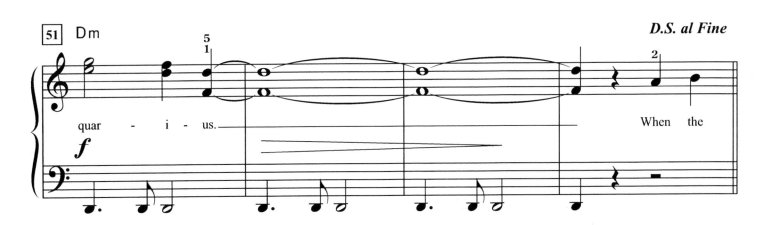

quar - i - us.——

f

When the

D.S. al Fine

AS TIME GOES BY

"As Time Goes By" was first composed for the little-known musical *Everybody's Welcome* (1931). However, its usage throughout the classic, romantic film *Casablanca* (1942) made it famous. *Casablanca* starred Humphrey Bogart as Rick, a conflicted nightclub owner, and Ingrid Bergman as Ilsa, Rick's former lover. "As Time Goes By" was "their song" and was performed in the film by Dooley Wilson who played Sam, Rick's nightclub pianist. *Casablanca* won three Academy Awards in 1943, including Best Picture.

Words and Music by Herman Hupfeld
Arranged by Dan Coates

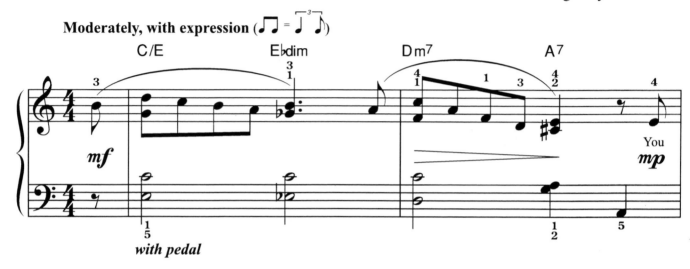

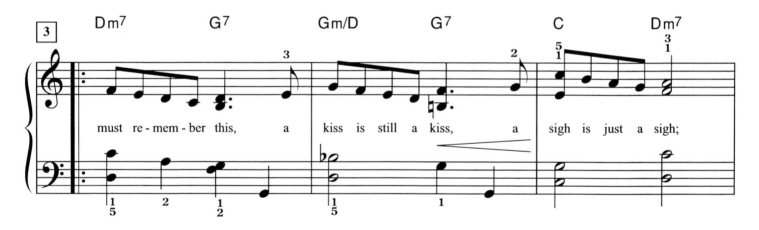

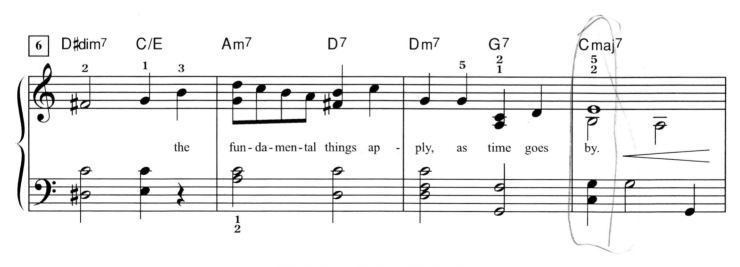

And when two lov-ers woo, they still say, "I love you," on

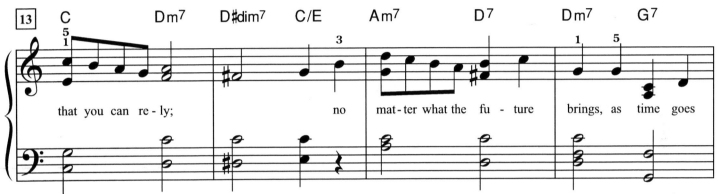

that you can re - ly; no mat-ter what the fu - ture brings, as time goes

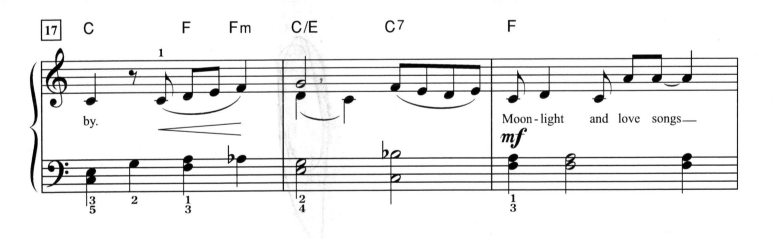

by. Moon-light and love songs—

nev - er out of date, hearts full of pas - sion,— jeal - ou - sy and hate;

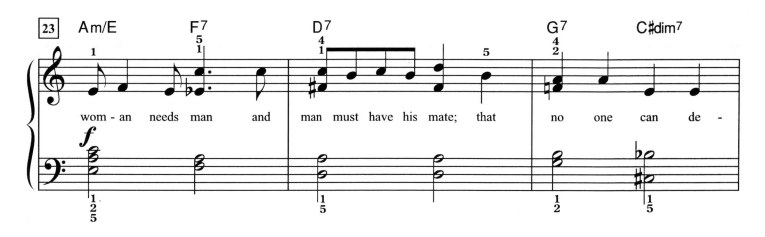

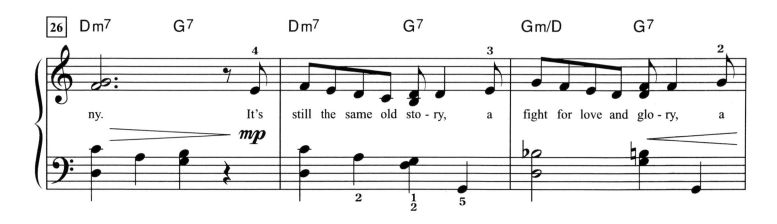

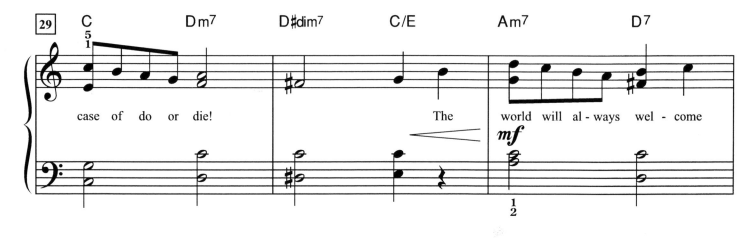

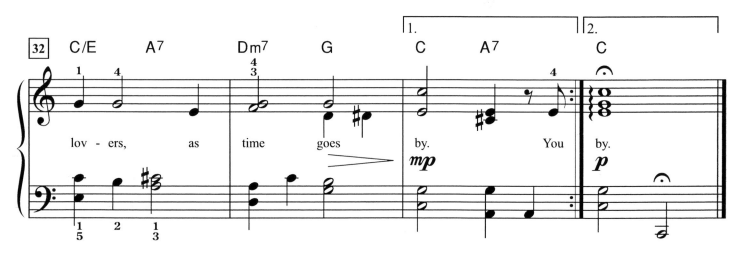

AT LAST

"At Last" was written by Mack Gordon and Harry Warren in 1941 and was a major hit for Glenn Miller and his band. However, the song is closely associated with Etta James, the famous R & B singer. In 1999 James was inducted into the Grammy Hall of Fame for her version of "At Last." It became her signature song and is frequently heard at weddings.

Music by Harry Warren
Lyric by Mack Gordon
Arranged by Dan Coates

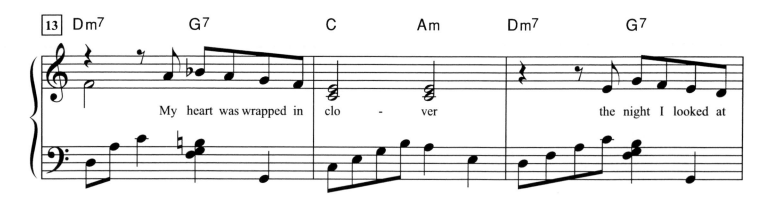

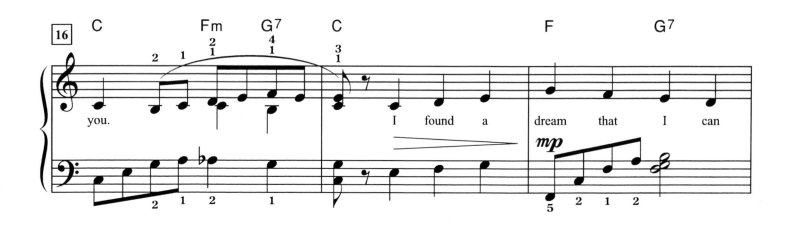

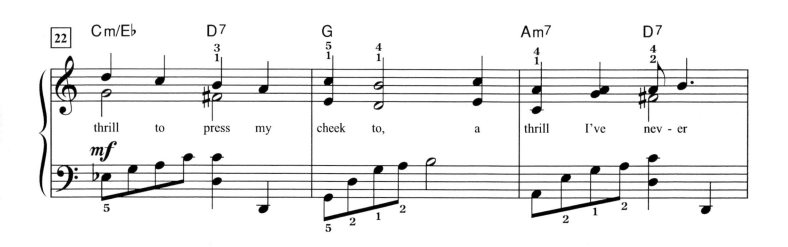

THE BALLAD OF GILLIGAN'S ISLE

CBS aired the hit sitcom *Gilligan's Island* between 1964 and 1967. The premise involved seven people of various social positions—a millionaire and his wife, a movie star, a professor, a farm girl, a ship captain and his first mate—shipwrecked on an uninhabited island somewhere in the middle of the Pacific Ocean. The title character has become one of America's top pop icons.

Words and Music by
Sherwood Schwartz and George Wyle
Arranged by Dan Coates

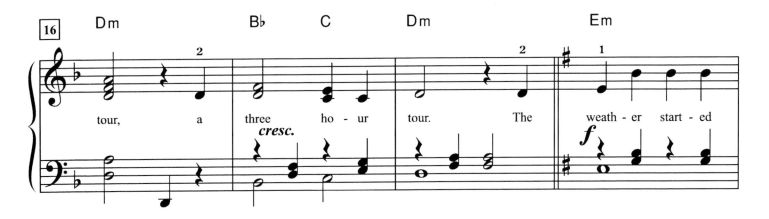

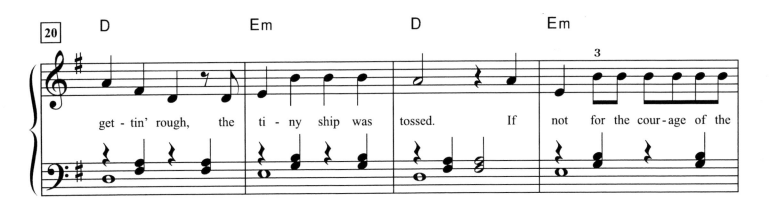

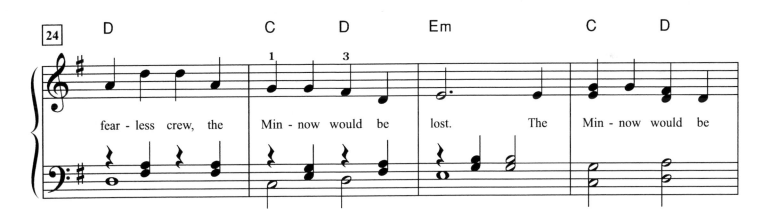

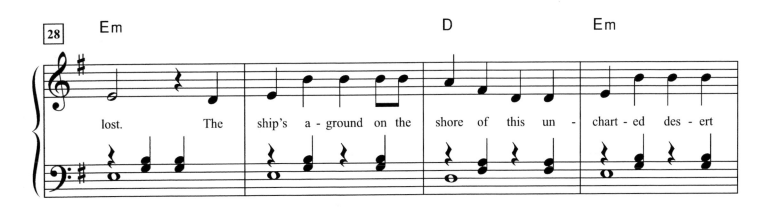

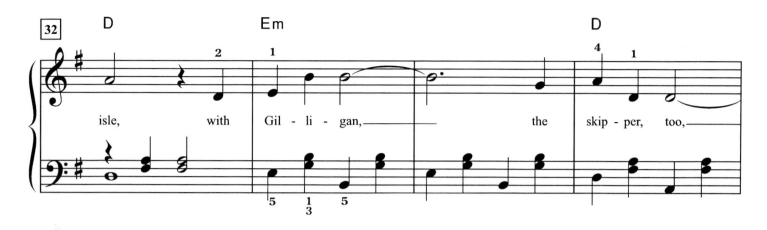

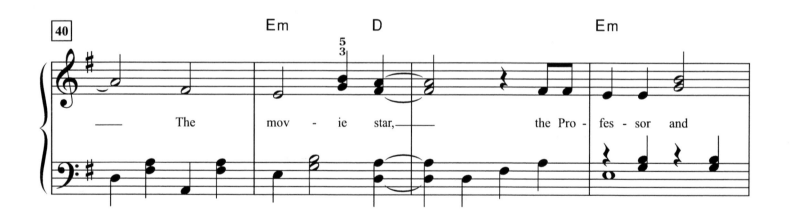

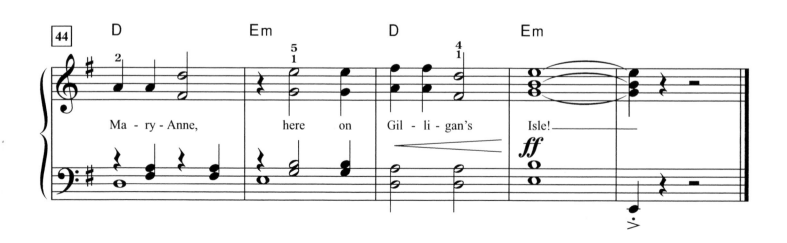

THE BEST IS YET TO COME

"The Best Is Yet to Come" has been recorded by many artists including Tony Bennett, Peggy Lee, Sarah Vaughan, Ella Fitzgerald, Michael Bublé and more. However, it is most often associated with Frank Sinatra. In fact, the words "The Best Is Yet to Come" are imprinted on Sinatra's tombstone.

Music by Cy Coleman
Lyric by Carolyn Leigh
Arranged by Dan Coates

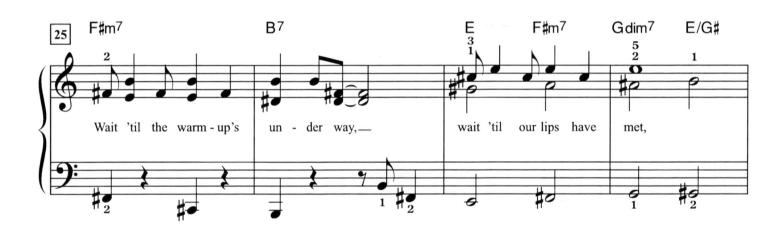

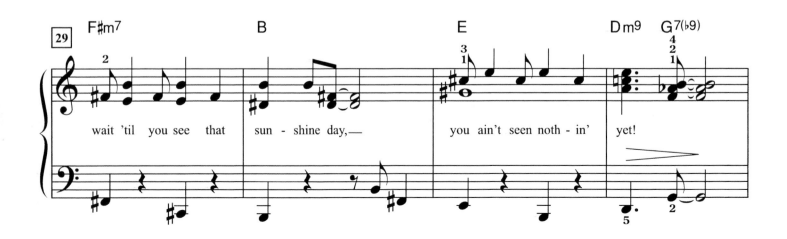

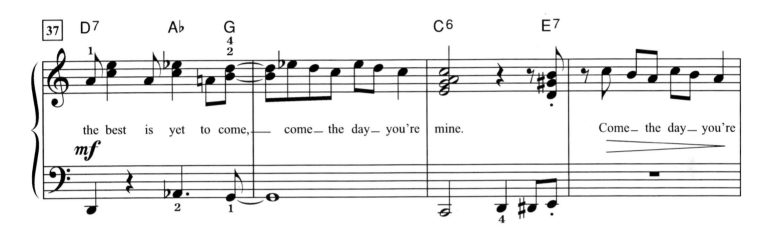

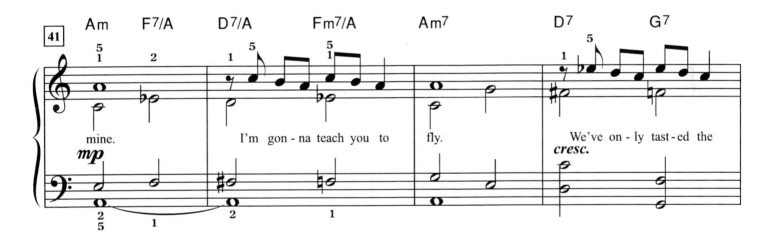

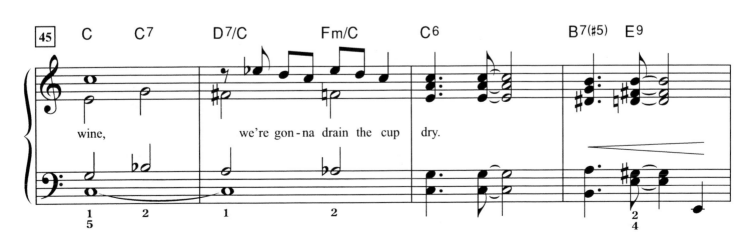

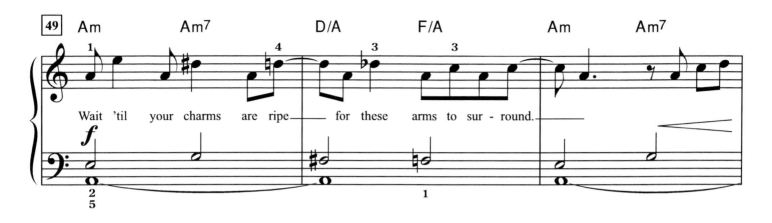

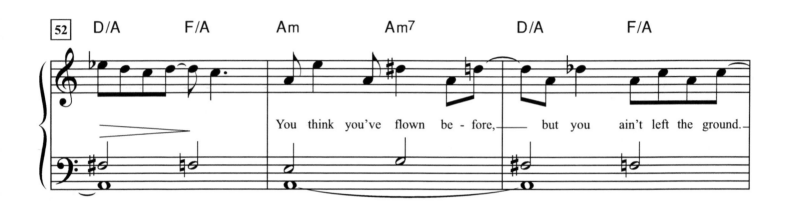

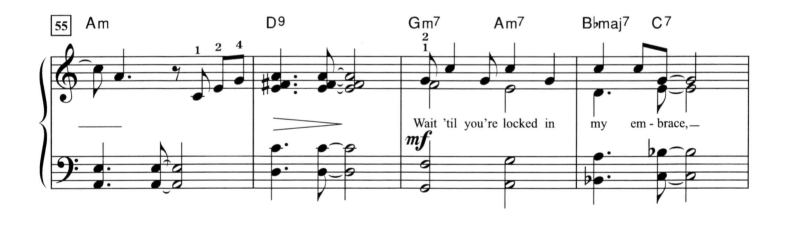

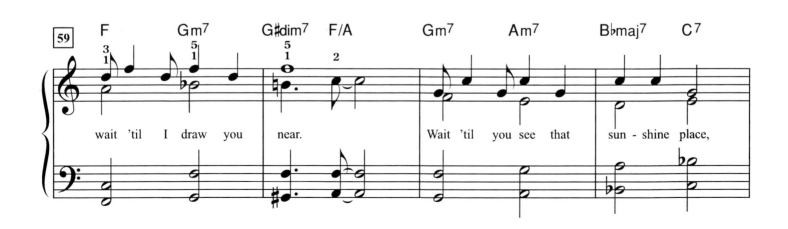

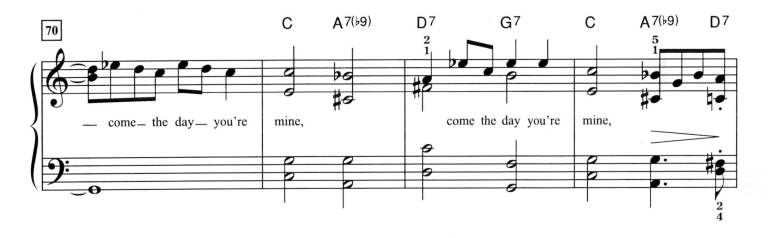

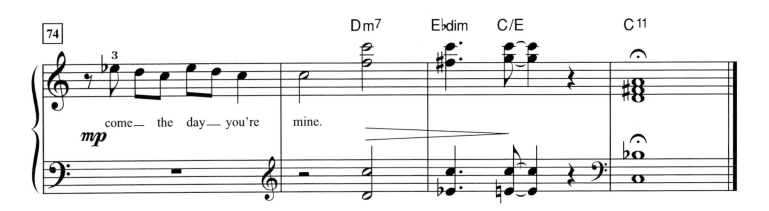

BRIDGE OVER TROUBLED WATER

Paul Simon and Art Garfunkel met in elementary school and performed in the same production of *Alice in Wonderland*. Years later they would collaborate as the duo Simon and Garfunkel and became known for their close vocal harmony, a sound reminiscent of The Everly Brothers. "Bridge Over Troubled Water" was their fifth and final studio album, which won five Grammy Awards. The title song stayed at the top of the Billboard Hot 100 for six weeks.

Words and Music by Paul Simon
Arranged by Dan Coates

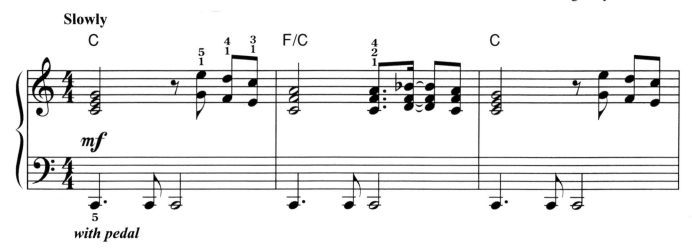

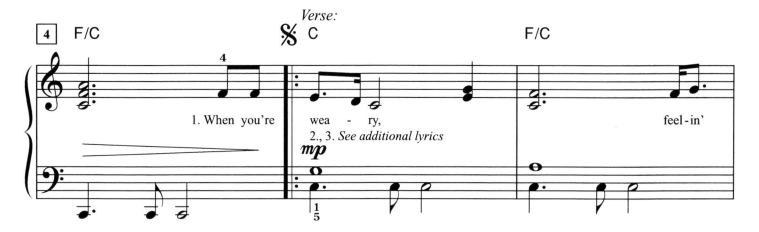

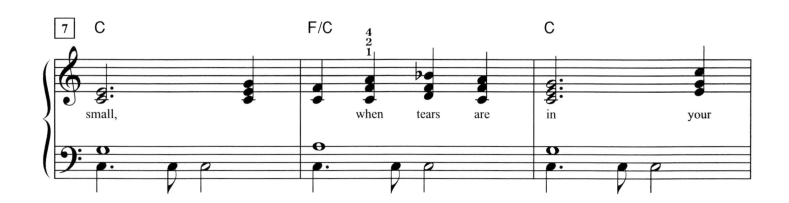

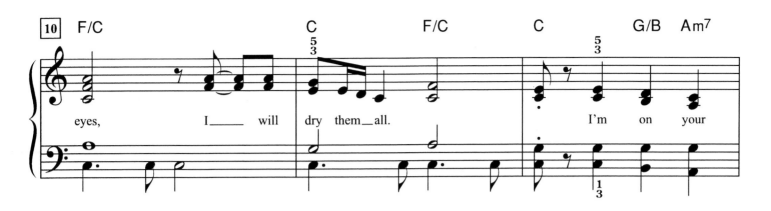

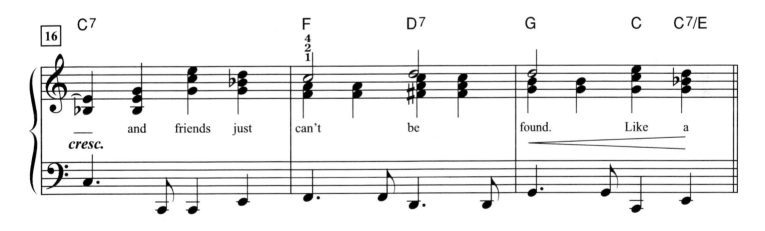

Chorus:

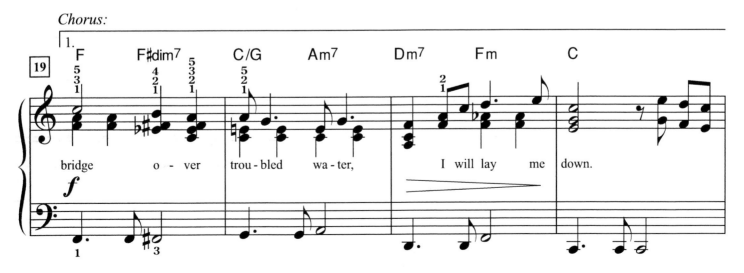

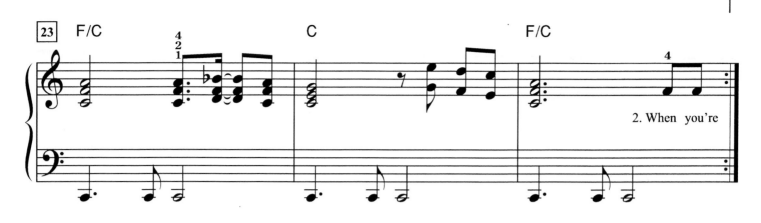

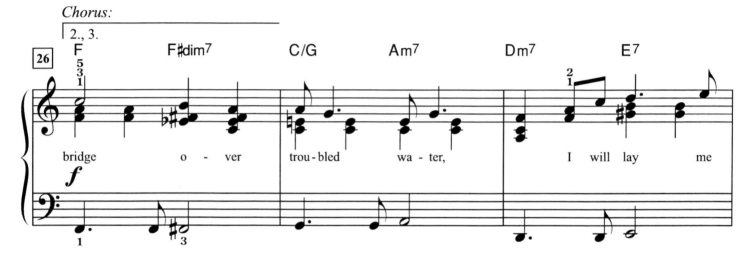

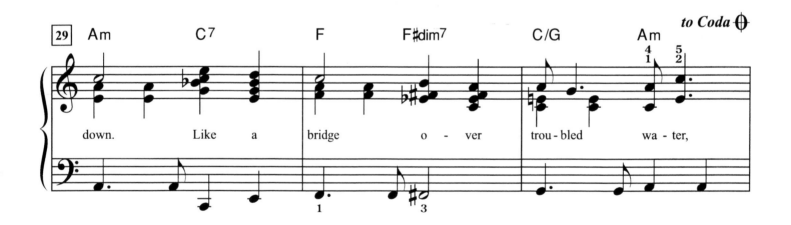

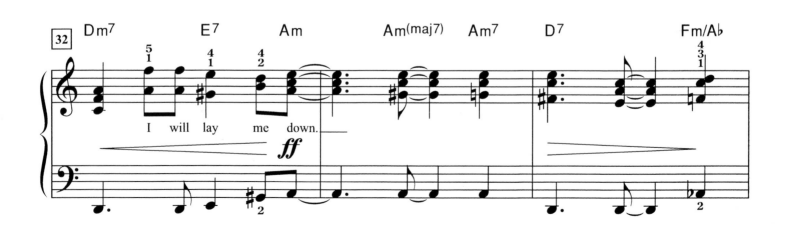

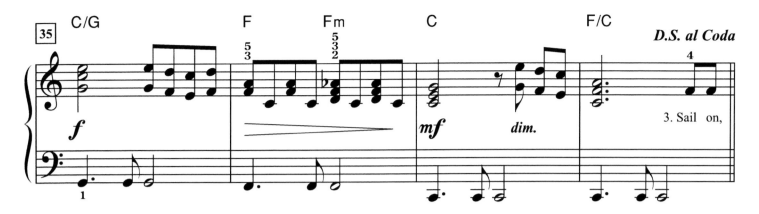

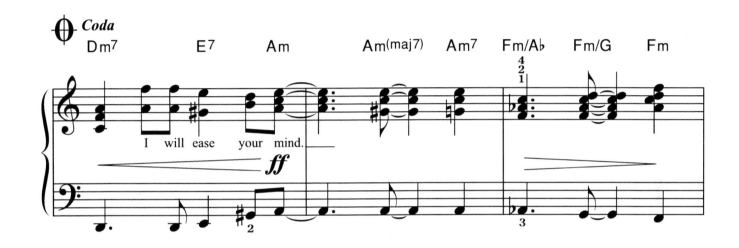

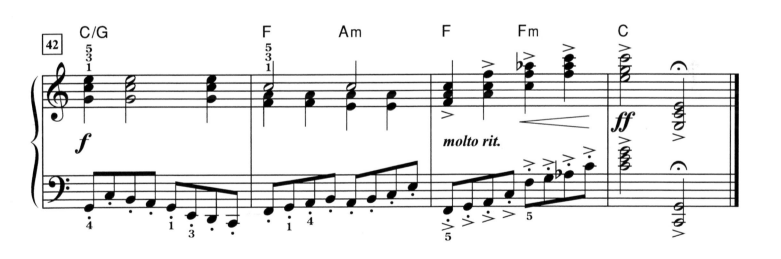

Verse 2:
When you're down and out,
When you're on the street,
When evening falls so hard, I will comfort you.
I'll take your part when darkness comes
And pain is all around.
Like a bridge over troubled water, I will lay me down.
Like a bridge over troubled water, I will lay me down.

Verse 3:
Sail on, silver girl, sail on by.
Your time has come to shine,
All your dreams are on their way.
See how they shine, if you need a friend.
I'm sailing right behind.
Like a bridge over troubled water, I will ease your mind.
Like a bridge over troubled water, I will ease your mind.

BLUE MOON

Though "Blue Moon" was penned in 1934 by Richard Rodgers and Lorenz Hart, perhaps the most famous version is the 1961 recording by The Marcels, a doo-wop group from Pittsburgh, Pennsylvania. Their up-tempo rendering of this classic ballad garnered a #1 hit, sold over a million copies, and earned a spot on the Rock and Roll Hall of Fame's "500 Songs that Shaped Rock and Roll" list.

Music by Richard Rodgers
Lyrics by Lorenz Hart
Arranged by Dan Coates

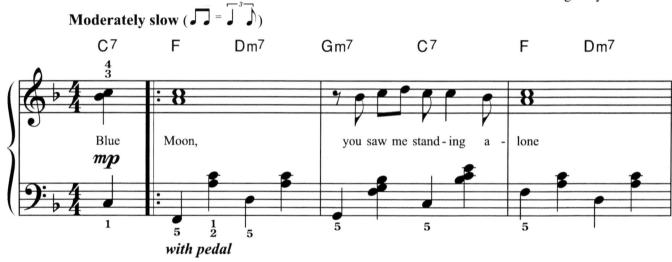

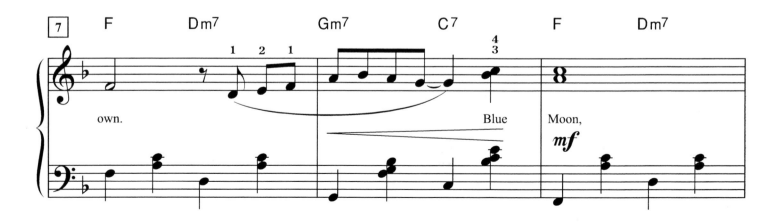

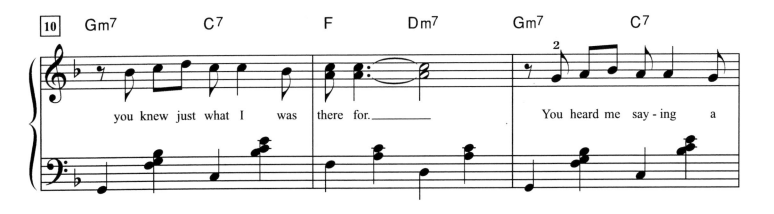

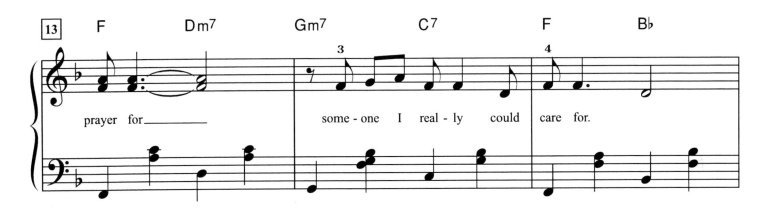

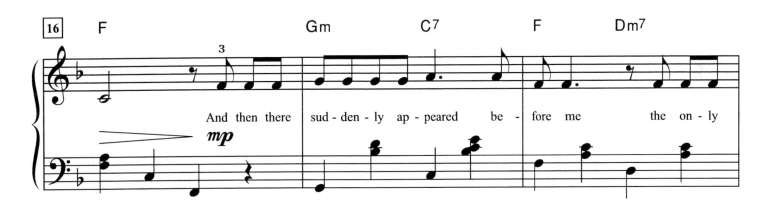

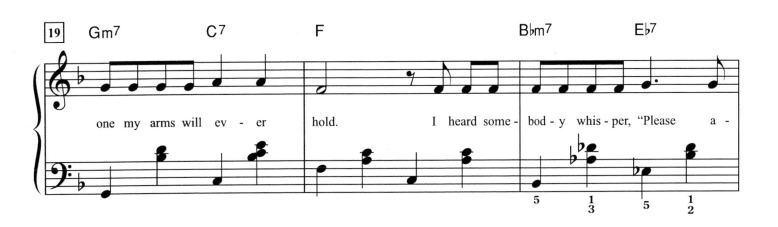

28

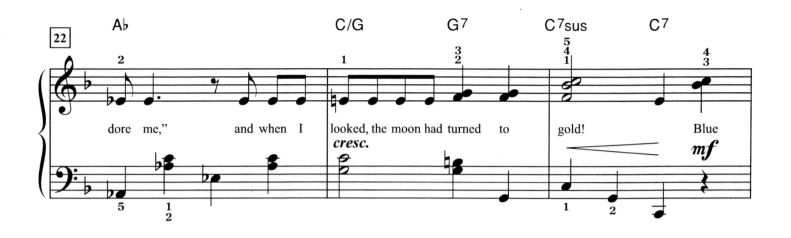

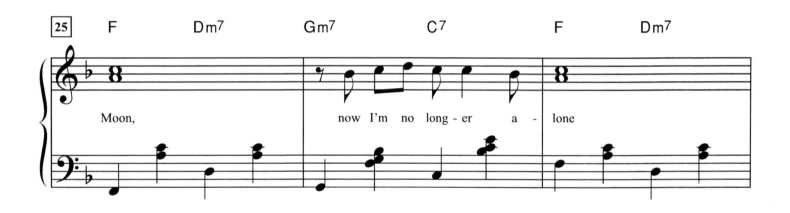

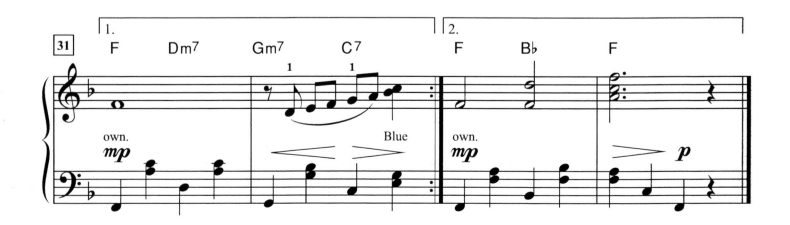

CAN YOU FEEL THE LOVE TONIGHT
(from Walt Disney's *The Lion King*)

The Lion King (1994) is Walt Disney's 32nd animated feature film and one of the highest-grossing animated films in history. The film won two Academy Awards: Best Original Score (Hans Zimmer) and Best Original Song for "Can You Feel the Love Tonight" (Elton John and Tim Rice). Elton John performed "Can You Feel the Love Tonight" for the closing credits of the film and won a Grammy Award for the performance.

Music by Elton John
Words by Tim Rice
Arranged by Dan Coates

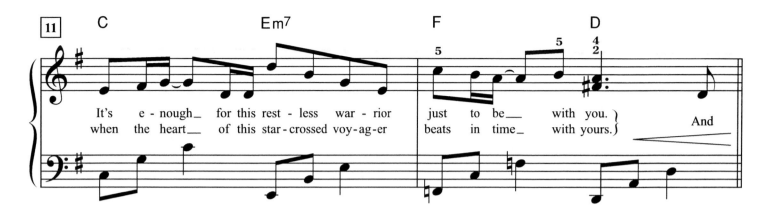

It's e-nough__ for this rest-less war-rior just to be__ with you.
when the heart__ of this star-crossed voy-ag-er beats in time__ with yours.
And

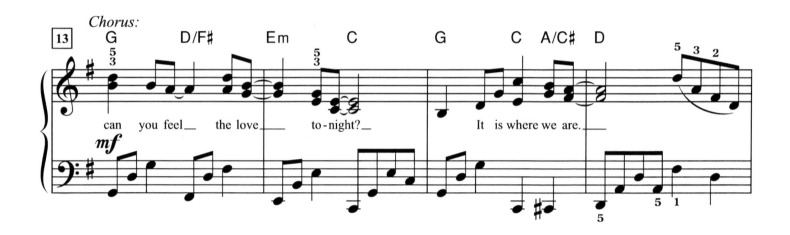

Chorus:

can you feel__ the love__ to-night?__ It is where we are.__

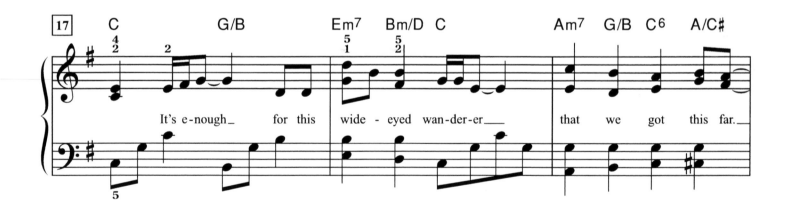

It's e-nough__ for this wide-eyed wan-der-er__ that we got this far.__

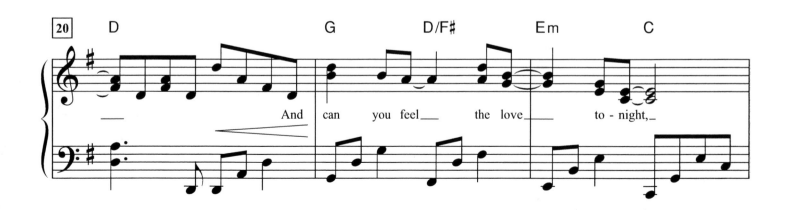

And can you feel__ the love__ to-night,__

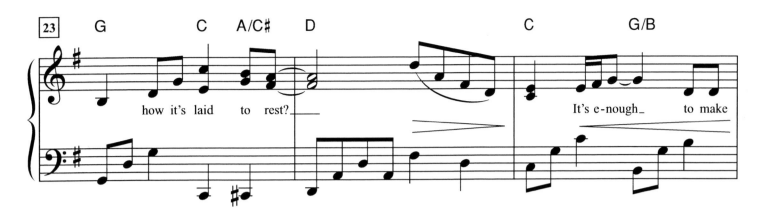

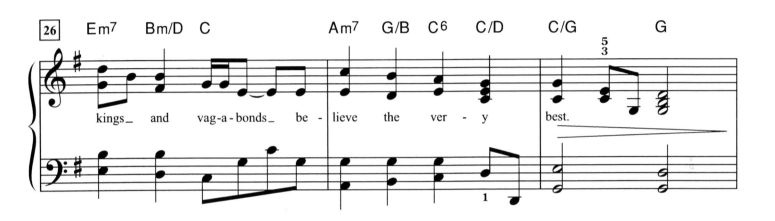

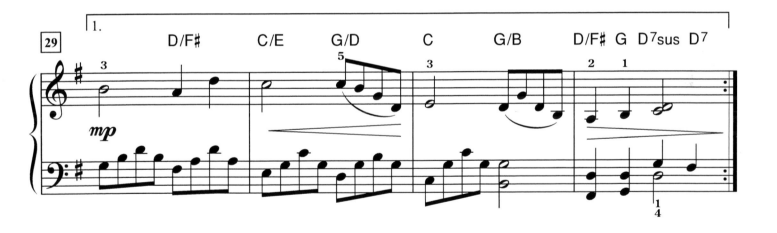

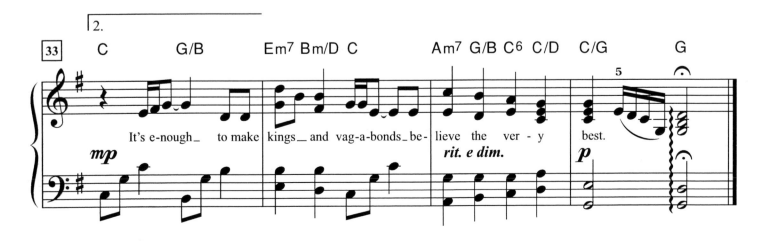

CRAZY FOR YOU

"Crazy for You" was Madonna's second #1 hit in the U.S. It was featured in the 1985 coming-of-age drama *Vision Quest*, starring Matthew Modine and Linda Fiorentino. In the movie, Madonna makes an appearance (her first in a major motion picture) as a singer at a local bar where she performs two songs: "Crazy for You" and "Gambler."

Words and Music by
John Bettis and Jon Lind
Arranged by Dan Coates

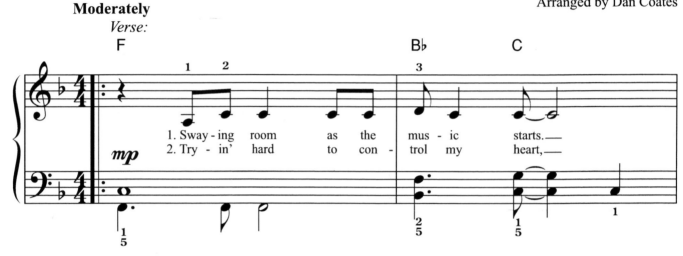

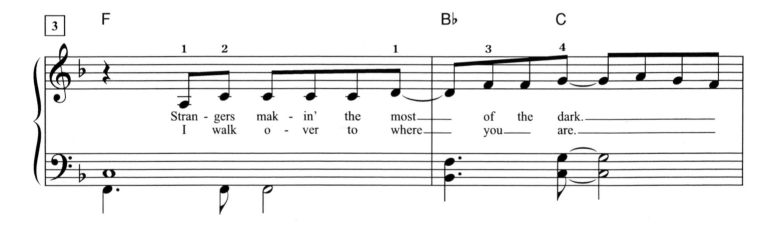

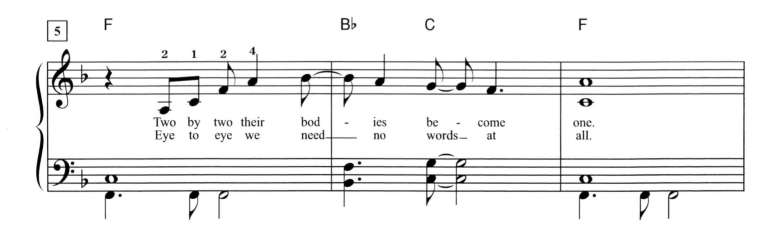

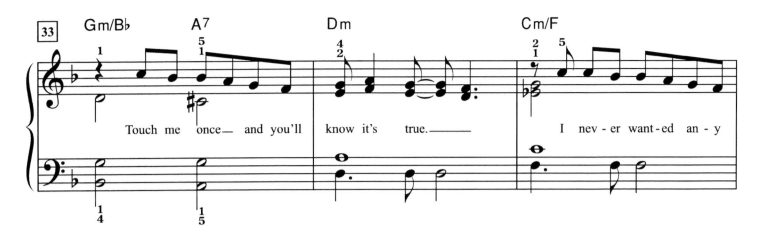

Touch me once— and you'll know it's true.——— I nev-er want-ed an-y

one like this.— It's all brand— new.— You'll feel it in my kiss.——

I'm cra-zy for you.——— Cra-zy for——

you, I'm cra-zy for—— you.

rit. e dim.

DANCING QUEEN

In 1975 the Swedish pop group, ABBA (an acronym for the first letters of the band members' names), recorded "Dancing Queen" on their album *Arrival*. It was released as a single the following year, reached the top of the charts internationally, and has become their signature song. Their pop/disco sound is quintessential of the '70s and can also be heard in their other hits: "Take a Chance on Me," "Super Trouper," and "S.O.S." to name a few.

Words and Music by Benny Andersson,
Stig Anderson and Bjorn Ulvaeus
Arranged by Dan Coates

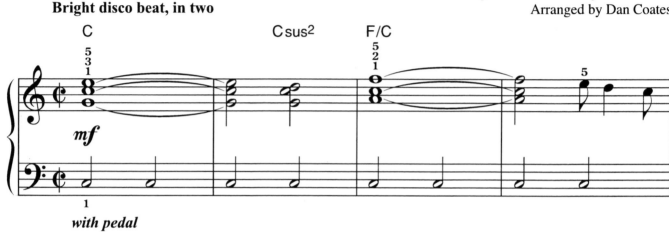

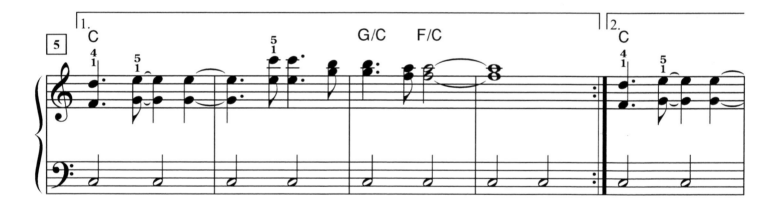

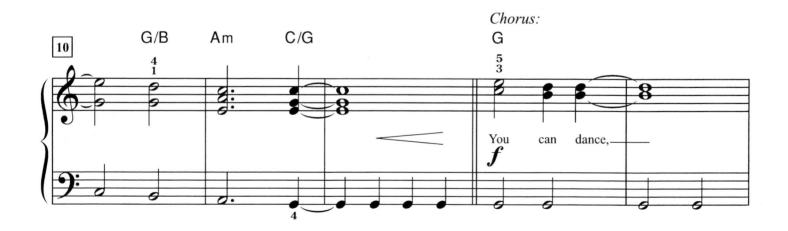

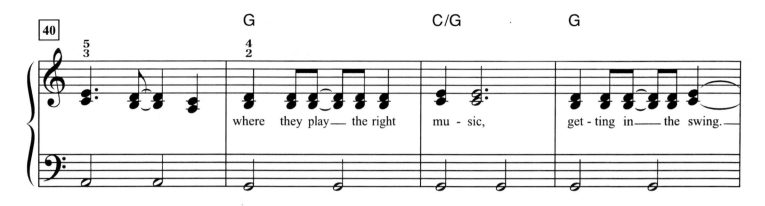

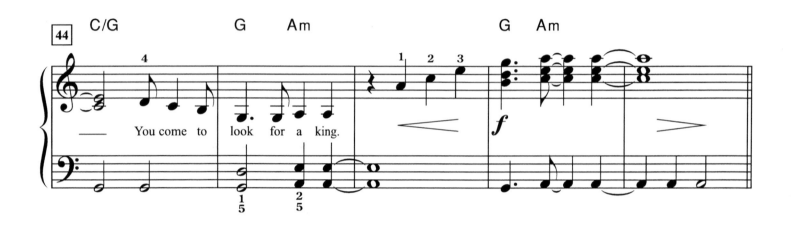

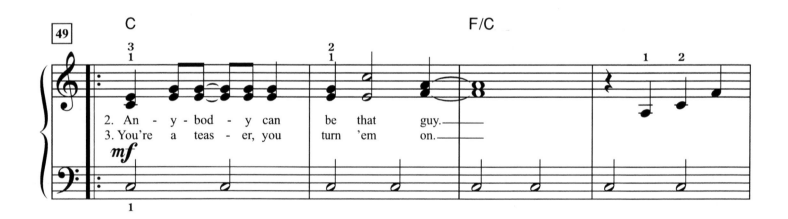

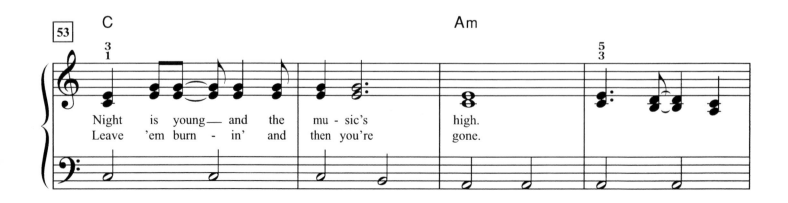

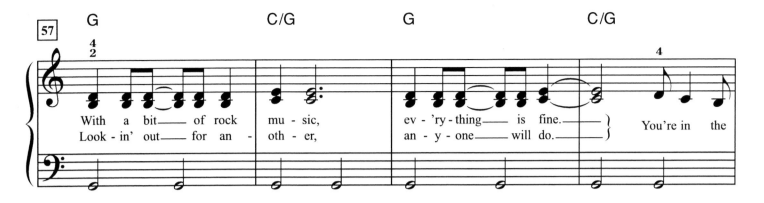

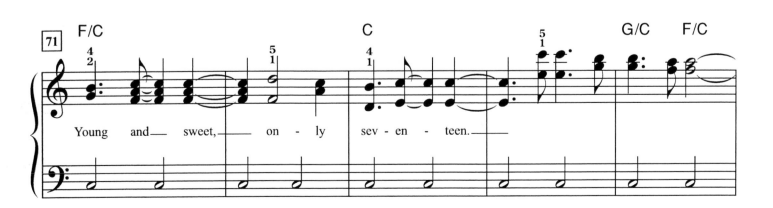

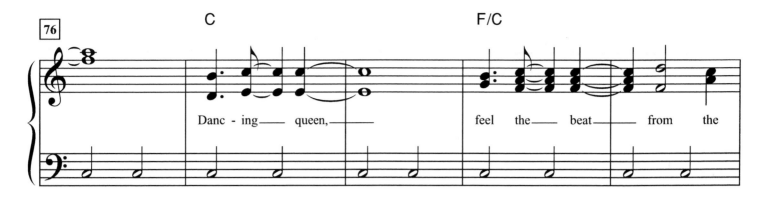

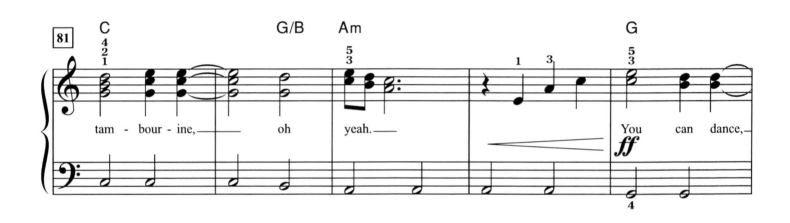

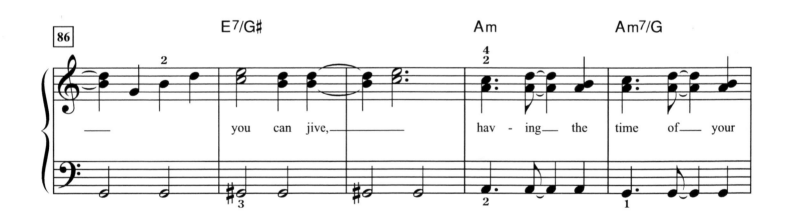

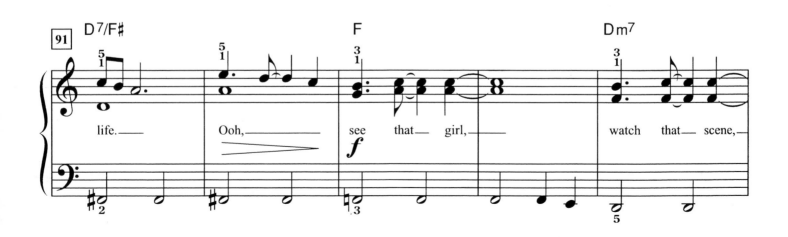

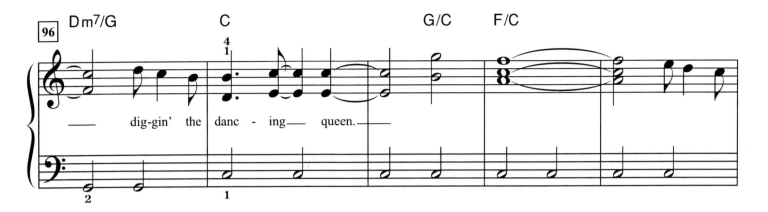

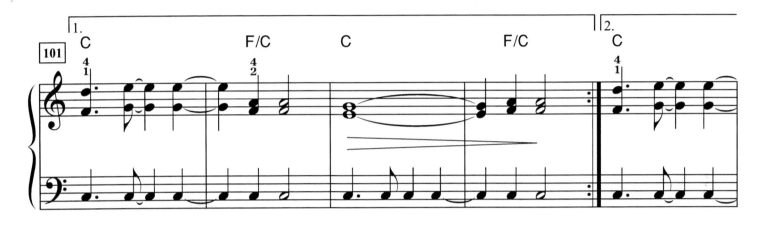

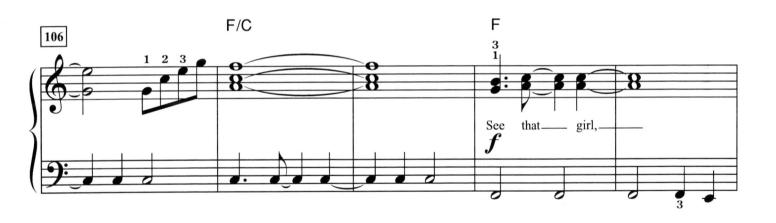

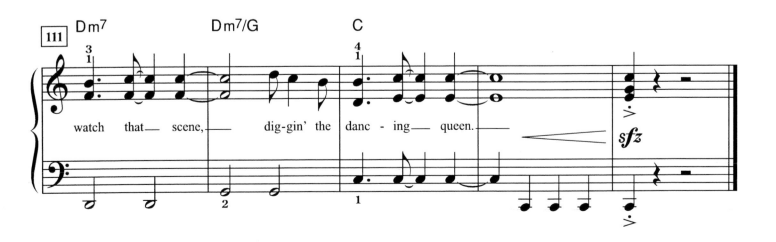

DANNY BOY

Frederic Weatherly, an English lawyer, author, lyricist, and broadcaster, wrote the lyrics for the ballad "Danny Boy" in 1913. However, the melody of the song was written much earlier. The first printing of the untitled tune was in an 1855 collection titled *The Petrie Collection of the Ancient Music of Ireland* (edited by George Petrie). It was collected by a Miss J. Ross from the county of Londonderry, Ireland, and has since been referred to as the "Londonderry Air."

Words and Music by Frederic Weatherly
Arranged by Dan Coates

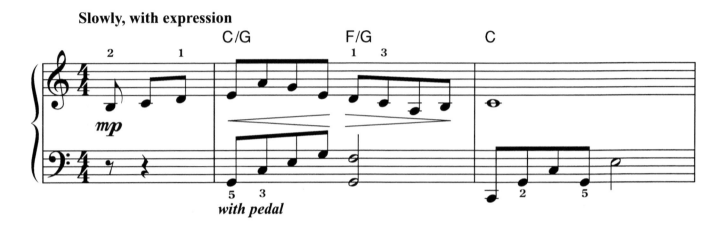

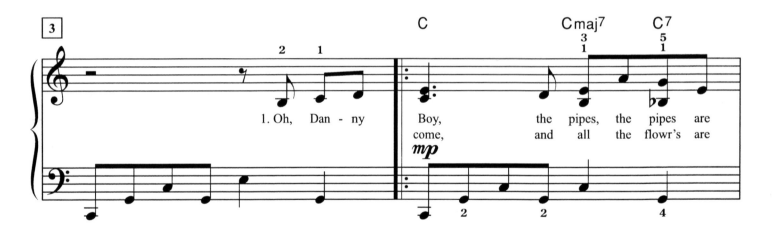

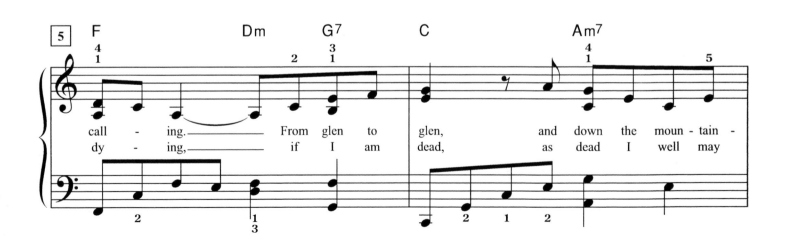

DON'T RAIN ON MY PARADE

If "People" is the great ballad from *Funny Girl*, "Don't Rain on My Parade" is *Funny Girl's* great up-tempo number. Barbra Streisand sang it both in the original Broadway production (1964) and in the film adaptation (1968). It is a particularly challenging song to sing with its fast, consonant-heavy lyrics in the verses, and with its huge, climactic, belty ending.

Music by Jule Styne
Words by Bob Merrill
Arranged by Dan Coates

Brightly, with a steady beat

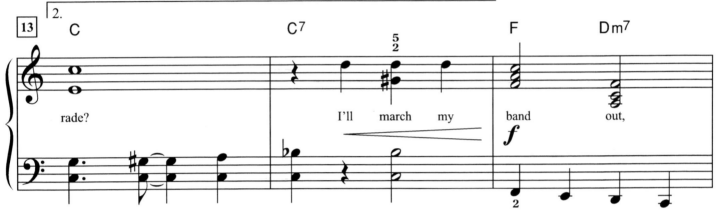

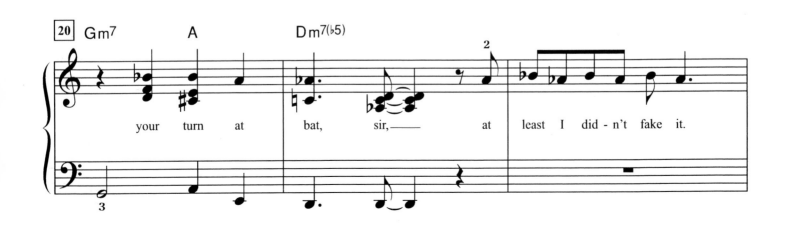

Hat, sir,— I guess I did-n't make it! But wheth - er I'm the

rose of sheer— per-fec - tion or freck - le on the nose of life's— com-plex-ion,

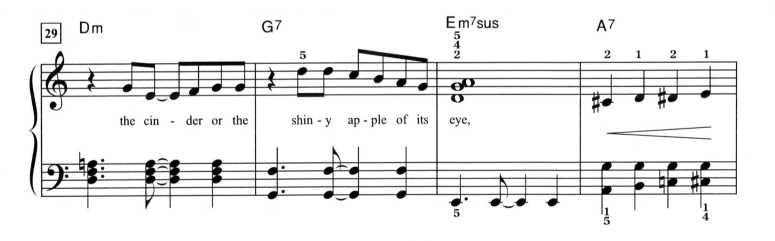

the cin - der or the shin - y ap-ple of its eye,

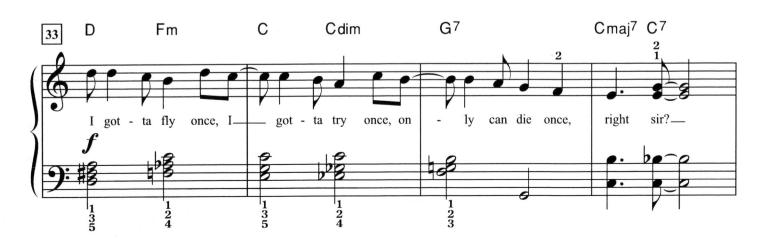

I got - ta fly once, I— got - ta try once, on - ly can die once, right sir?—

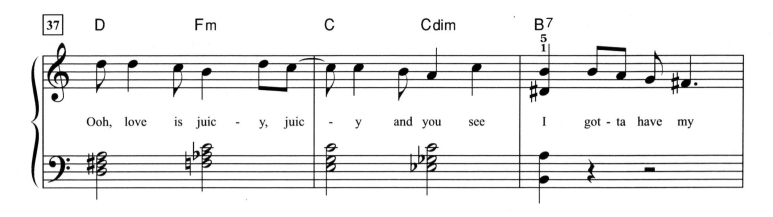

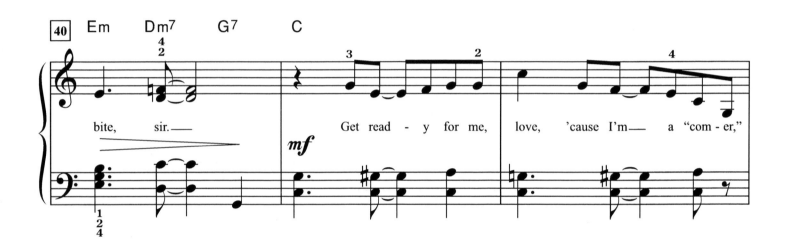

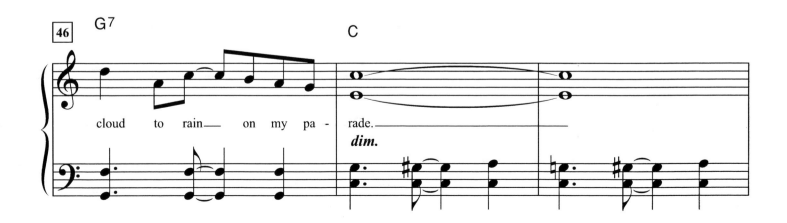

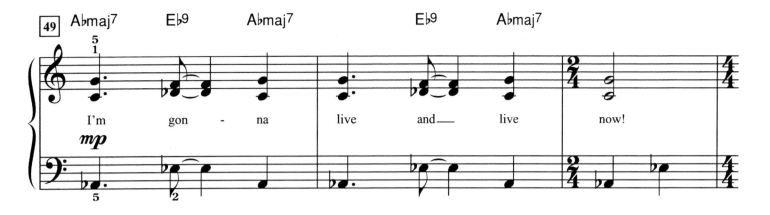

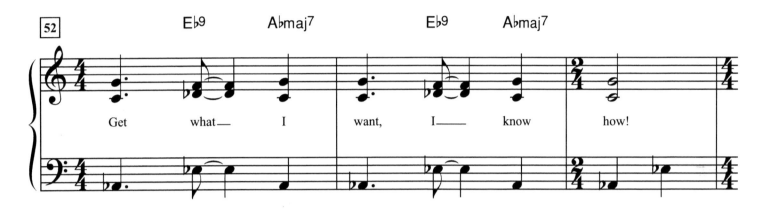

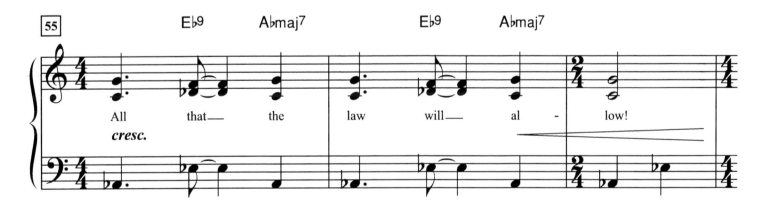

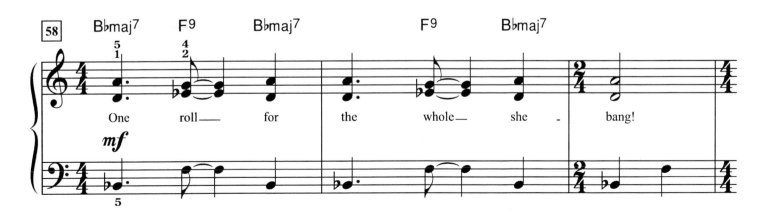

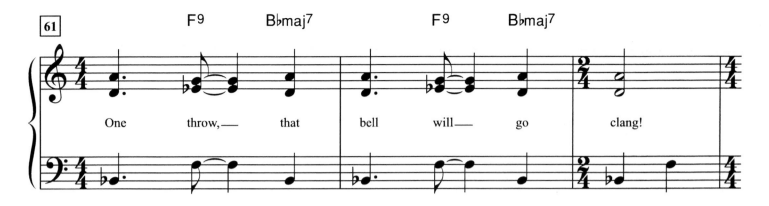

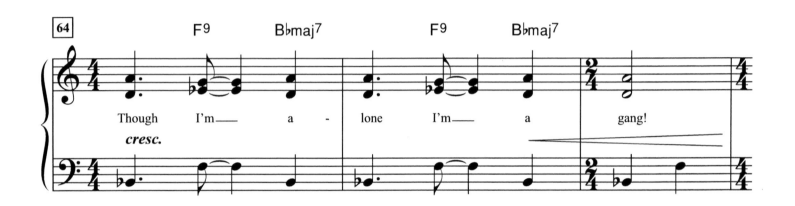

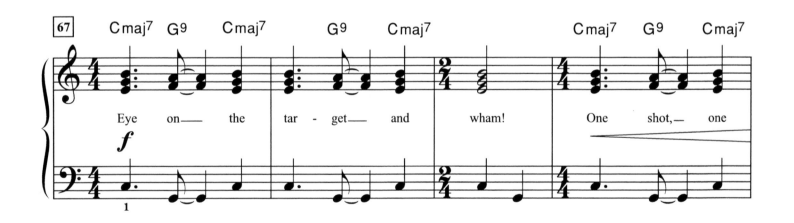

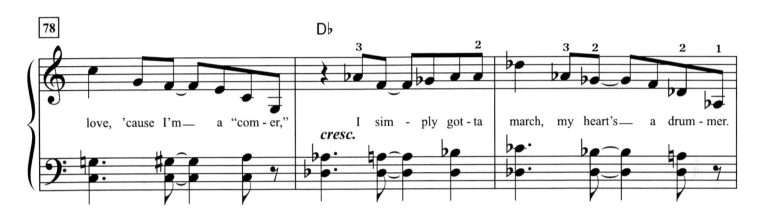

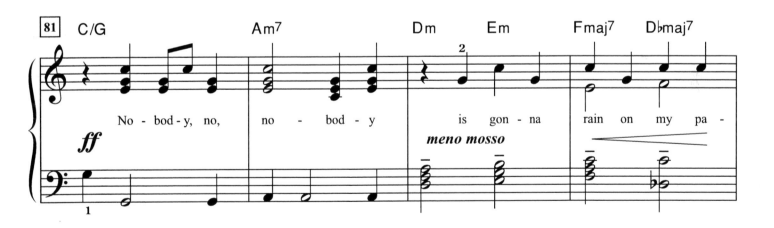

DESPERADO

"Desperado" first appeared on the 1973 Eagles album of the same name. *Desperado* was a concept album based on the Dalton Gang, outlaws of the Old West. Although "Desperado" was never released as a single, it has become one of their signature songs. It also has been covered by numerous artists including Linda Ronstadt, The Carpenters, Clint Black, Johnny Cash, Carrie Underwood, and The Dixie Chicks.

Words and Music by
Don Henley and Glenn Frey
Arranged by Dan Coates

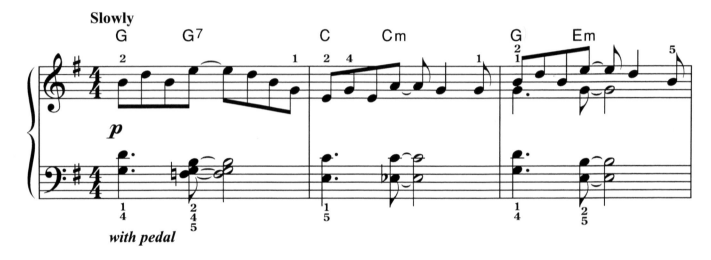

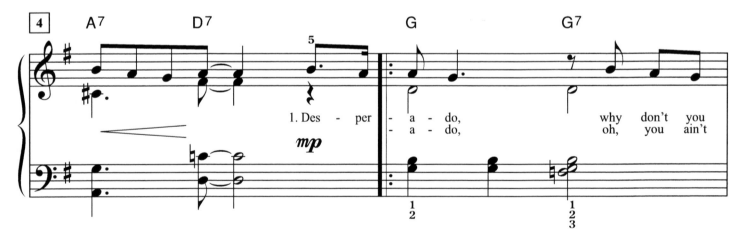

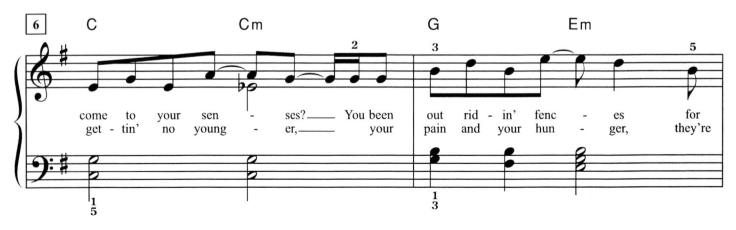

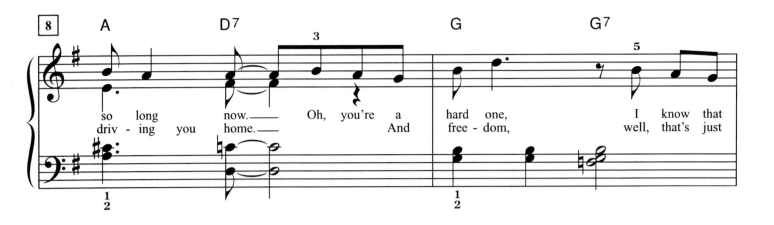

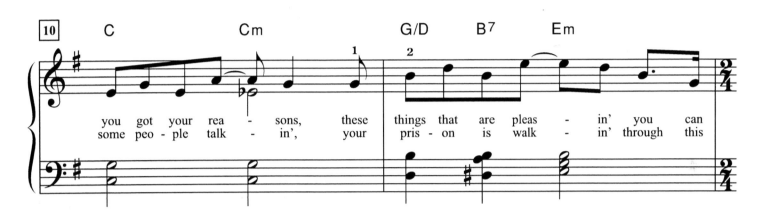

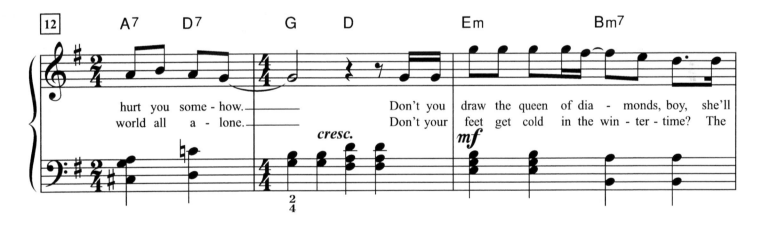

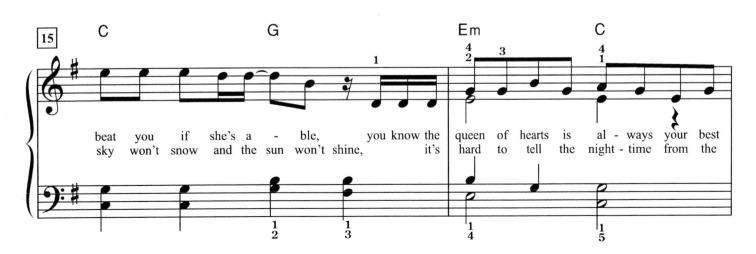

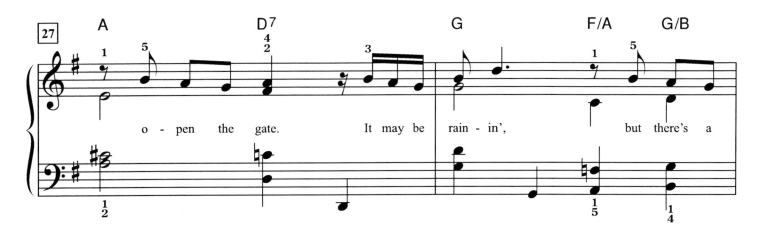

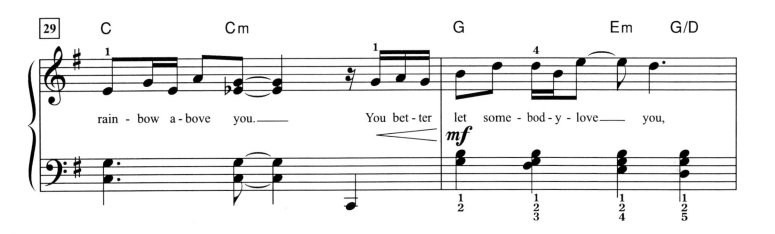

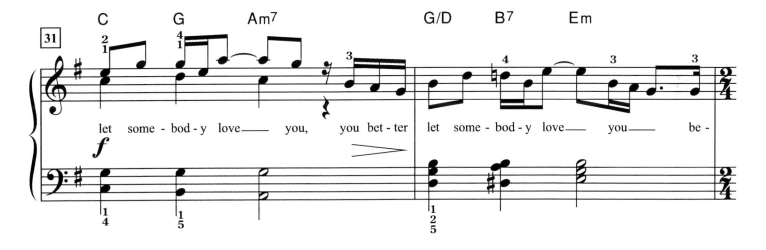

DON'T SIT UNDER THE APPLE TREE

"Don't Sit under the Apple Tree" was written for the musical film *Private Buckaroo* in 1942 and was made famous by The Andrews Sisters. The Andrews Sisters were a close-harmony singing group from Minnesota that became the best-selling female vocal group in pop music history. In addition to great success selling records, starring in Hollywood films, and making guest appearances on radio and television shows, they entertained troops regularly during World War II. "Don't Sit under the Apple Tree" is the story of a couple separated by the war.

Words and Music by
Charlie Tobias, Lew Brown and Sam H. Stept
Arranged by Dan Coates

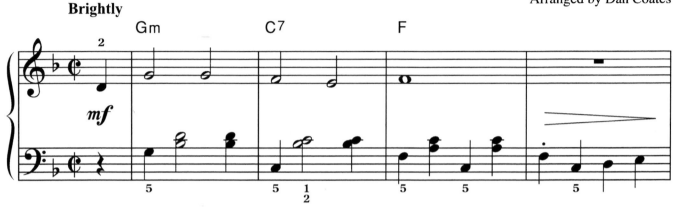

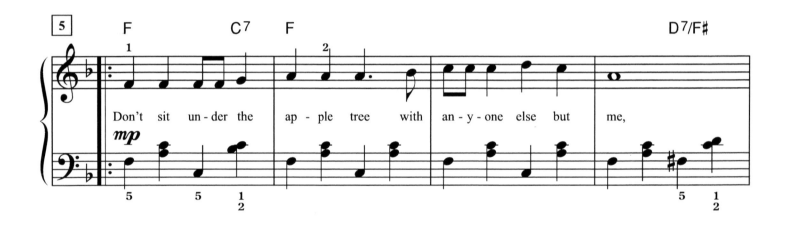

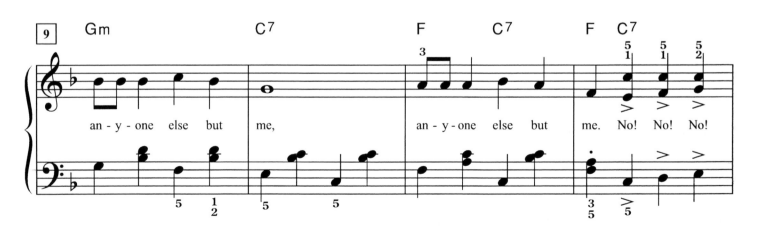

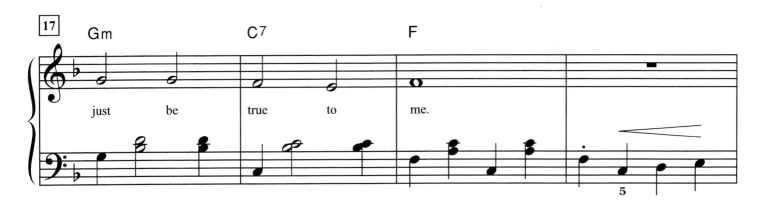

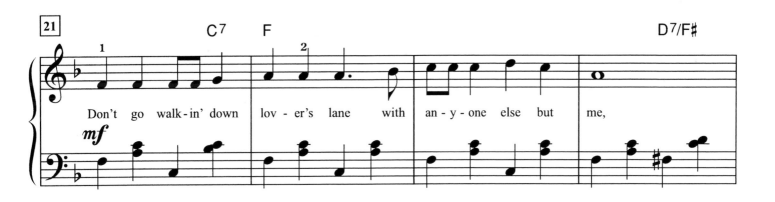

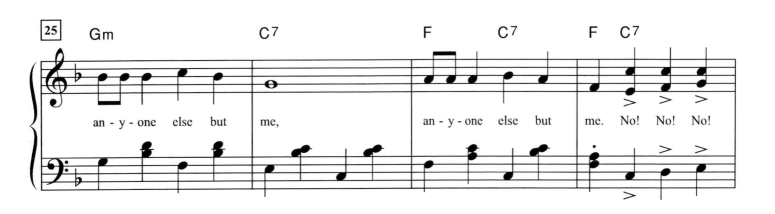

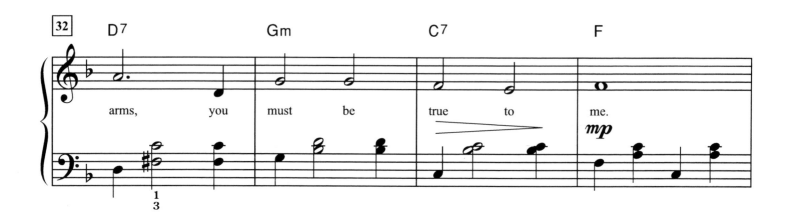

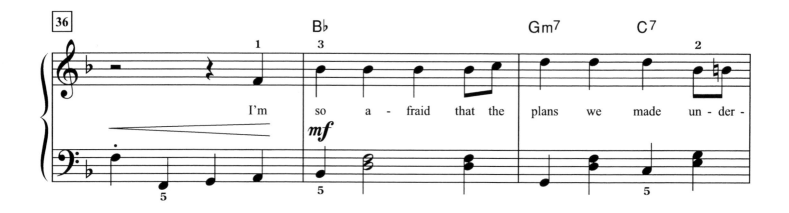

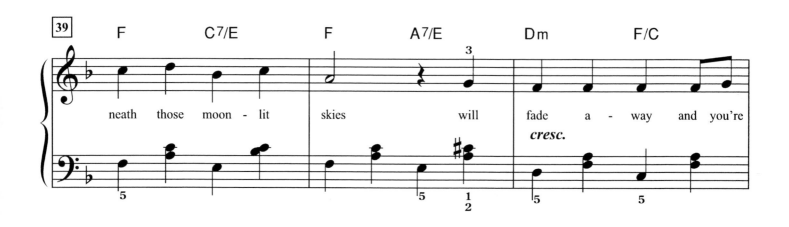

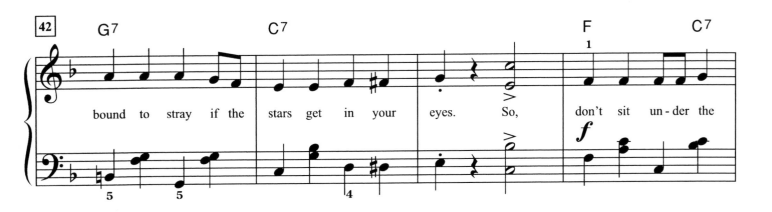

42 G7 C7 F C7

bound to stray if the stars get in your eyes. So, don't sit un-der the

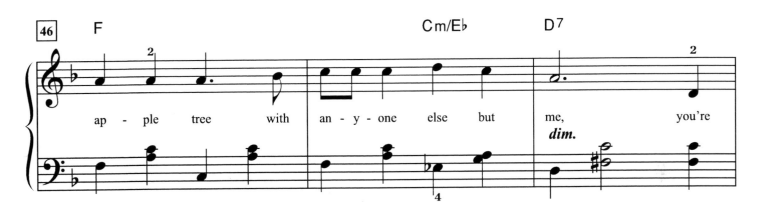

46 F Cm/E♭ D7

ap - ple tree with an - y - one else but me, *dim.* you're

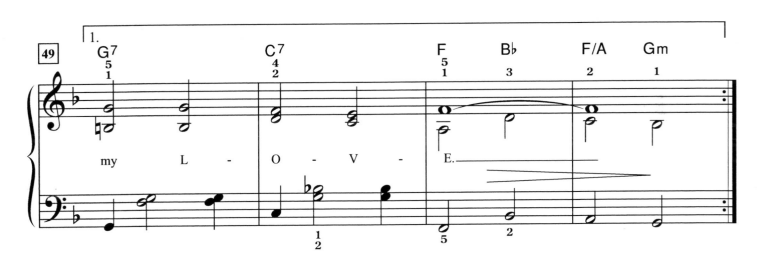

1.

49 G7 C7 F B♭ F/A Gm

my L - O - V - E.

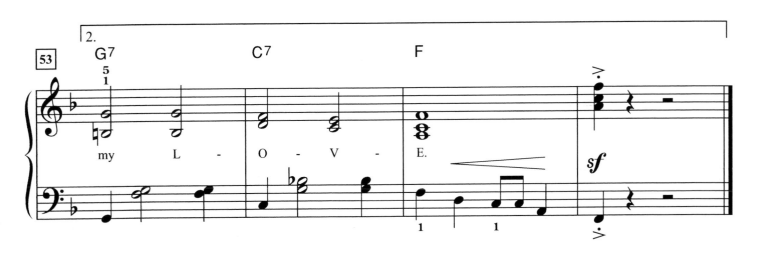

2.

53 G7 C7 F

my L - O - V - E. *sf*

DON'T STOP BELIEVIN'

While most smash-hit songs inevitably fade from popularity over time, this 1981 Top 10 single by American rock band Journey has extraordinary staying power. Three decades after its debut, "Don't Stop Believin'" remains inescapable on radio, television, in movies, and even at sporting events. It continues to rank impressively on numerous sales and popularity charts around the globe, and is particularly well-suited to be played on the piano.

Words and Music by
Jonathan Cain, Neal Schon and Steve Perry
Arranged by Dan Coates

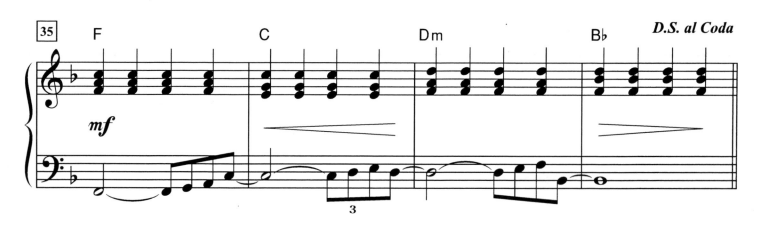

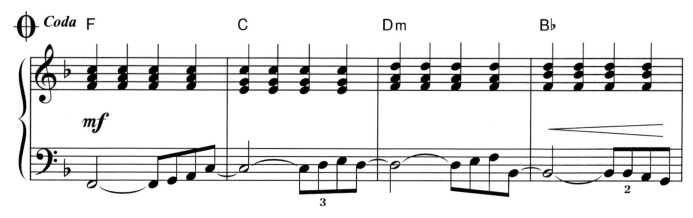

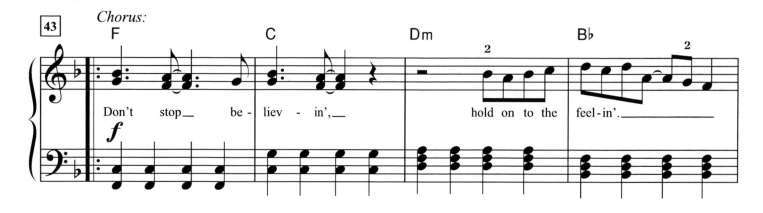

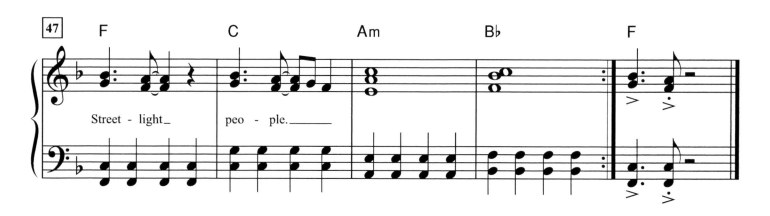

Verse 3:
A singer in a smoky room,
The smell of wine and cheap perfume.
For a smile they can share the night
It goes on and on and on and on.

Verse 4:
Working hard to get my fill.
Everybody wants a thrill,
Payin' anything to roll the dice
Just one more time.

Verse 5:
Some will win and some will lose,
Some were born to sing the blues.
Oh, the movie never ends,
It goes on and on and on and on.

ENDLESS LOVE

Soul singer Diana Ross and pop singer Lionel Richie recorded "Endless Love" in 1981 for the romantic drama of the same name. The movie was directed by Franco Zeffirelli and starred Brooke Shields and Martin Hewitt. The film was a commercial failure, but the song became the biggest-selling single of the year and has become one of the most popular duet ballads of all time. It was covered by Luther Vandross and Mariah Carey in 1994.

Words and Music by Lionel Richie
Arranged by Dan Coates

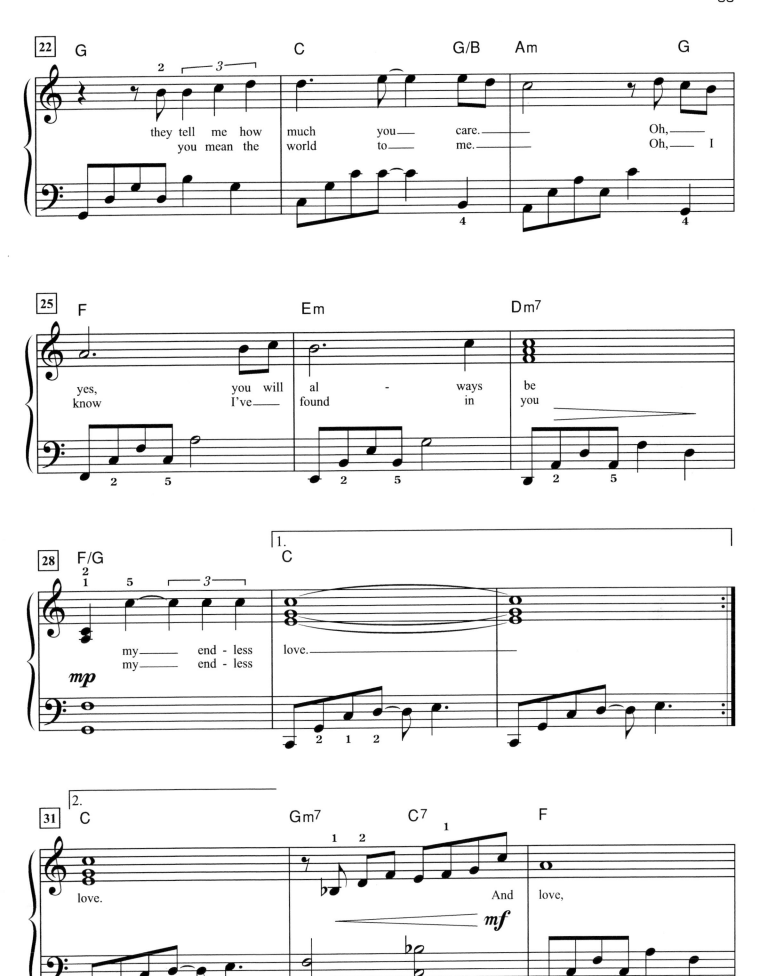

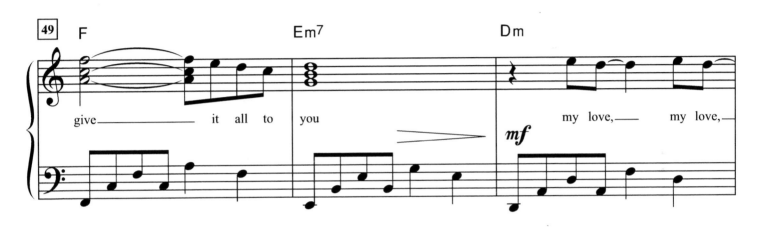

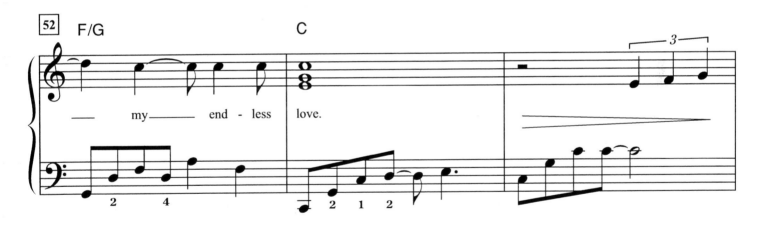

EYE OF THE TIGER

Sylvester Stallone asked the rock band Survivor to write a theme song for *Rocky III* (1982), the third of six movies about a boxer from Philadelphia. "Eye of the Tiger" was the result and became a smash hit, topping the Billboard Hot 100 for six weeks and winning a Grammy Award. The title of the hard rock anthem was based on a line from the movie's script, which had been written by Stallone.

Words and Music by
Frankie Sullivan III and Jim Peterik
Arranged by Dan Coates

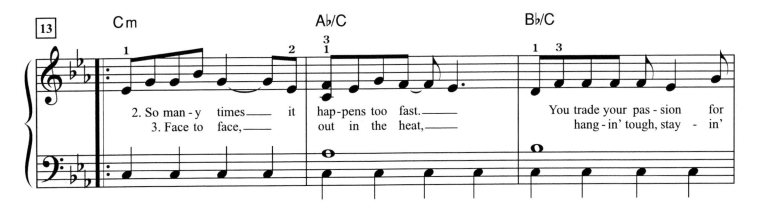

13

Cm   A♭/C   B♭/C

2. So man-y times___ it hap-pens too fast.___ You trade your pas-sion for
3. Face to face,___ out in the heat,___ hang-in' tough, stay - in'

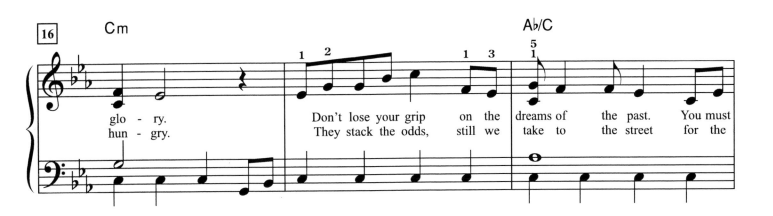

16

Cm   A♭/C

glo - ry. Don't lose your grip on the dreams of the past. You must
hun - gry. They stack the odds, still we take to the street for the

19

B♭/C   Cm   B♭   Cm   Fm

Chorus:

fight just to keep them a - live. It's the eye of the ti-ger. It's the
kill with the will to sur - vive.

f

22

E♭/G   B♭   Cm   Fm   Cm   B♭   Cm

thrill of the fight, ris - in' up to the chal-lenge of our ri - val. And the

70

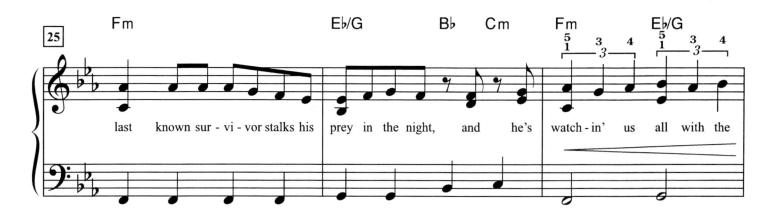

last known sur‑vi‑vor stalks his prey in the night, and he's watch‑in' us all with the

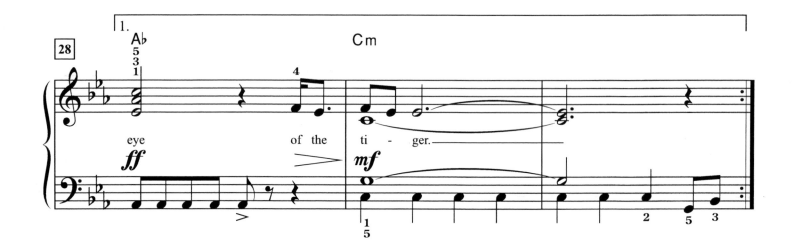

eye of the ti‑ger.

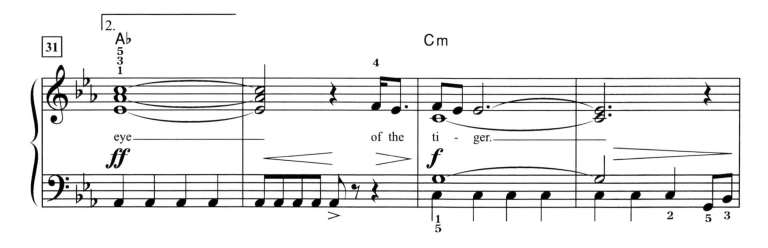

eye of the ti‑ger.

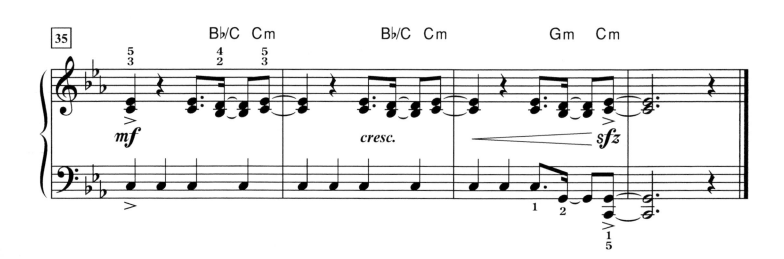

FALLING SLOWLY
(FROM *ONCE*)

The soundtrack for the 2007 independent film *Once* took the Grammy and Academy awards by storm with nominations for Best Original Song and Soundtrack. "Falling Slowly" won the Academy award for Best Original Song and was performed live at the ceremony by co-stars Glen Hansard and Markéta Irglová. In the movie, they played struggling musicians who cross paths at a crucial time in their lives.

Words and Music by
Glen Hansard and Marketa Irglova
Arranged by Dan Coates

Slowly, with expression

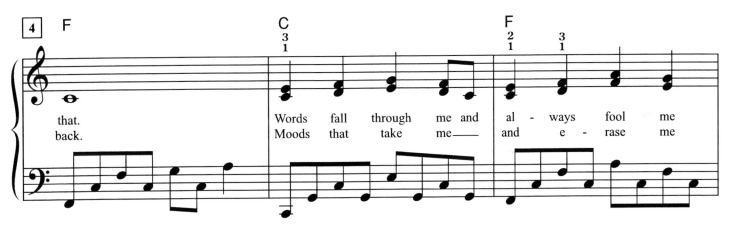

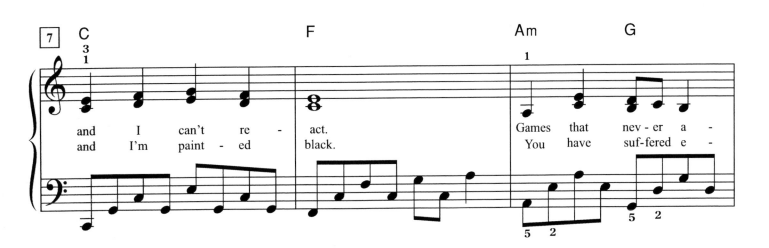

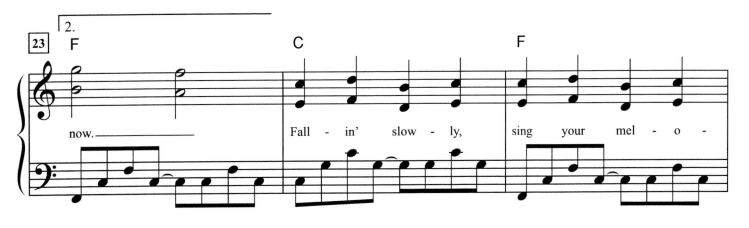

now.———— Fall - in' slow - ly, sing your mel - o -

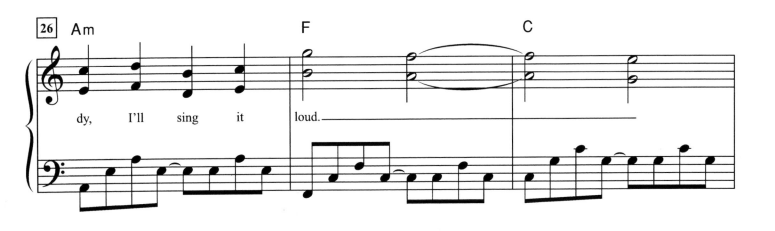

dy, I'll sing it loud.————

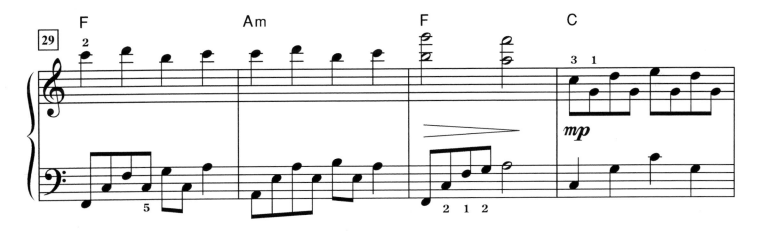

dim.   p   rit. e dim.   pp

GIVE MY REGARDS TO BROADWAY
(WWI version)

George M. Cohan was a multi-talented vaudeville performer when he was a boy. He acted, sang, danced, and even played violin. Between 1890 and 1901, he toured with his parents and sister in a family act called The Four Cohans. His love for performing continued as he grew older, and he went on to write, produce, and perform in dozens of Broadway shows. His first production was *Little Johnny Jones*, which featured the popular song "Give My Regards to Broadway."

Words and Music by George M. Cohan
Arranged by Dan Coates

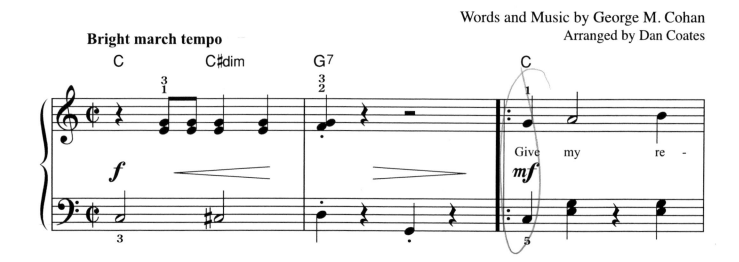

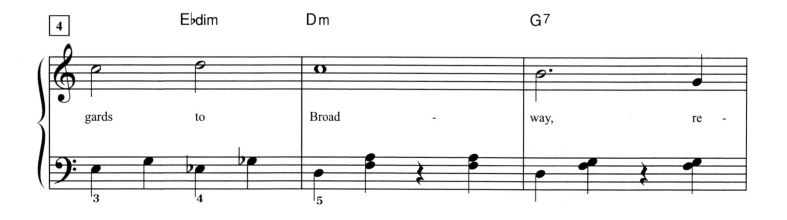

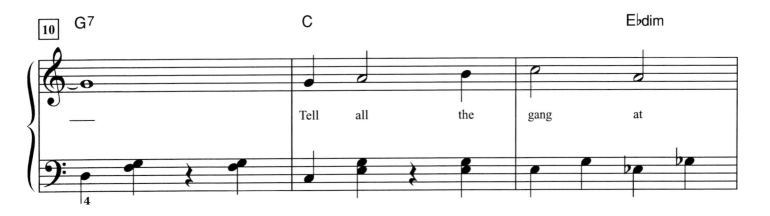

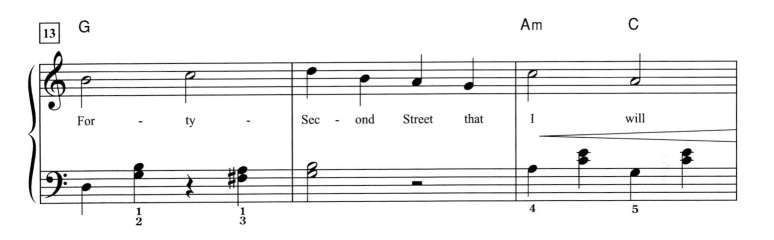

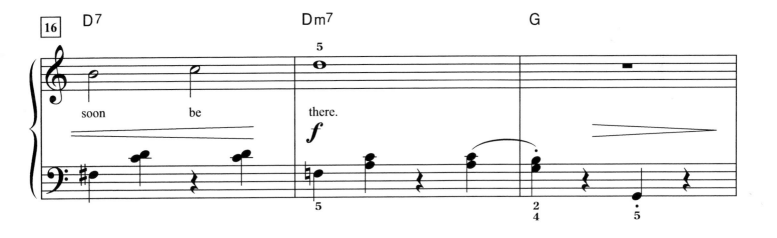

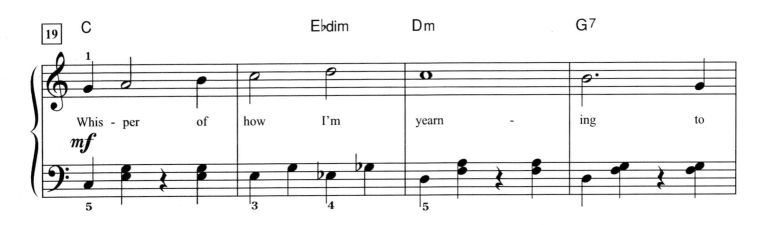

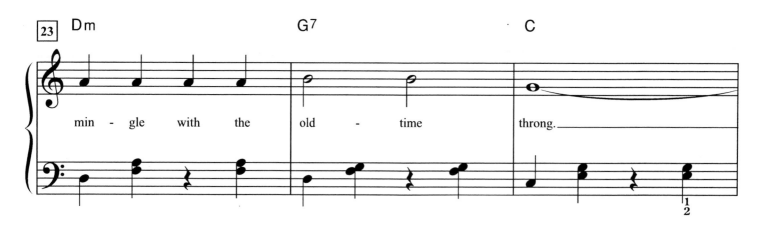

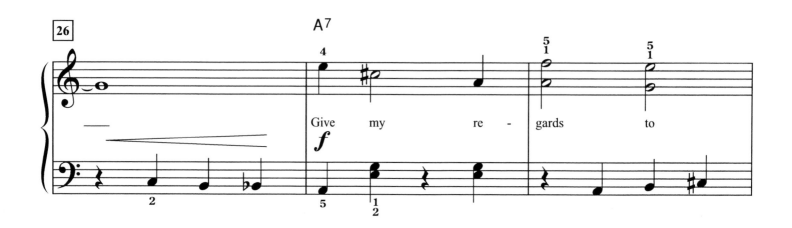

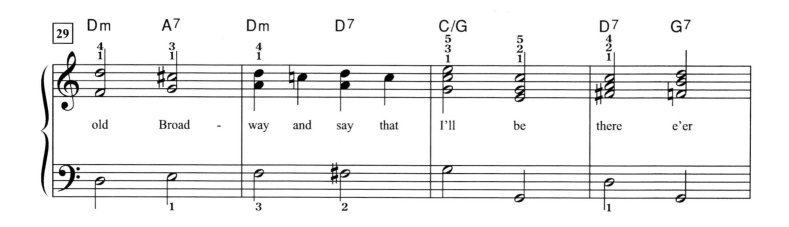

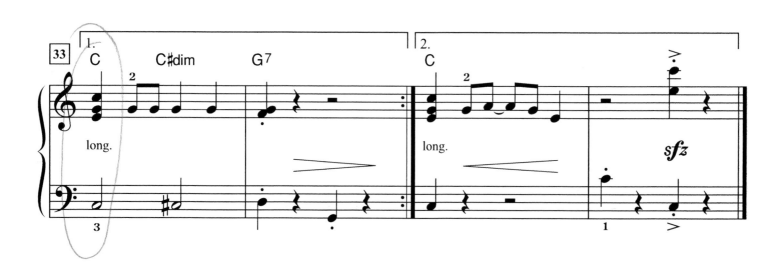

THE GREATEST LOVE OF ALL

George Benson recorded "The Greatest Love of All" for *The Greatest*, a 1977 film which starred boxing legend Muhammad Ali as himself. Linda Creed wrote the lyrics amidst a struggle with breast cancer; the words reflect her feelings about coping with the disease and being a young mother. Whitney Houston covered the song in 1986 on her self-titled debut album, a record which would eventually sell over 13 million copies and become one of the best-selling female debut albums in history.

Words by Linda Creed
Music by Michael Masser
Arranged by Dan Coates

Slowly, with expression

Verse:

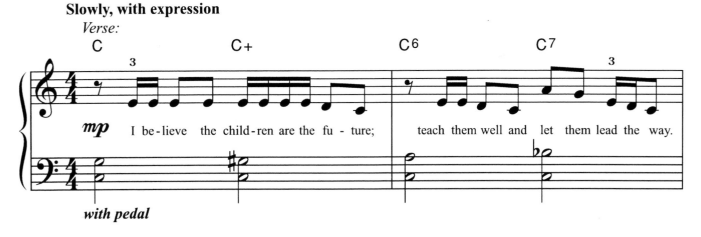

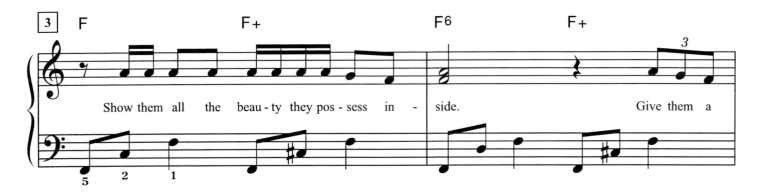

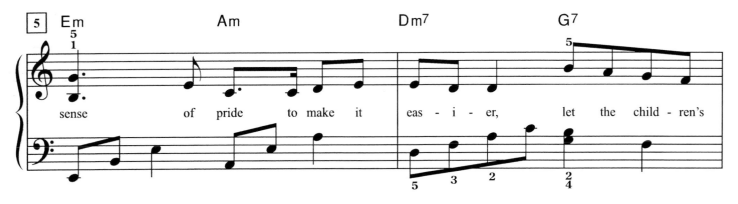

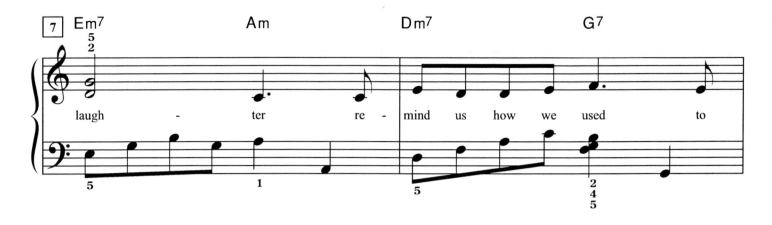

laugh - ter re - mind us how we used to

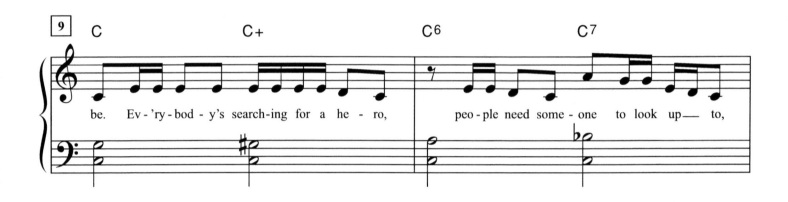

be. Ev - 'ry-bod - y's search-ing for a he - ro, peo - ple need some - one to look up — to,

I nev - er found an - y - one who ful - filled that need; a lone - ly

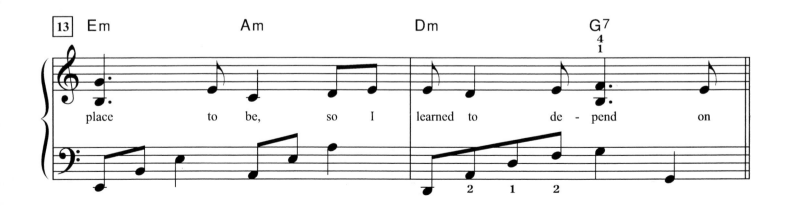

place to be, so I learned to de - pend on

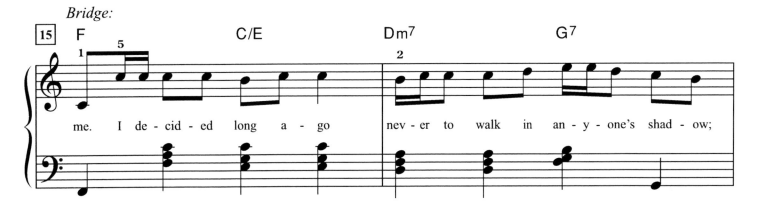

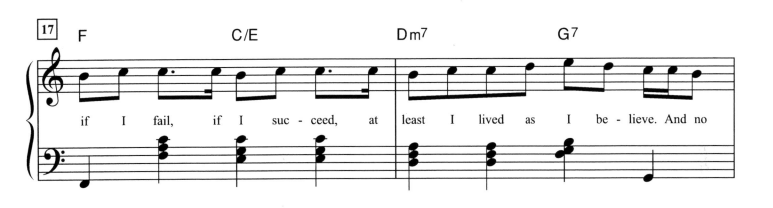

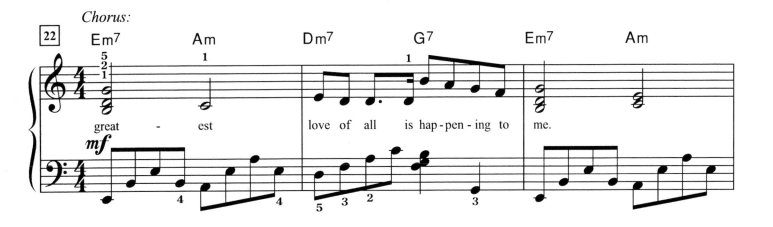

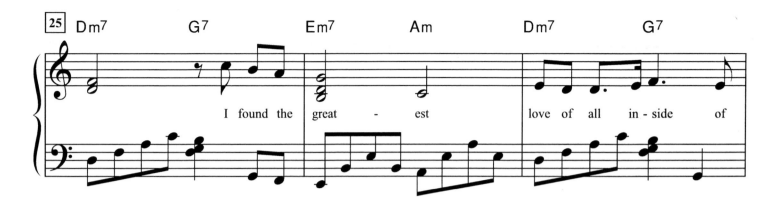

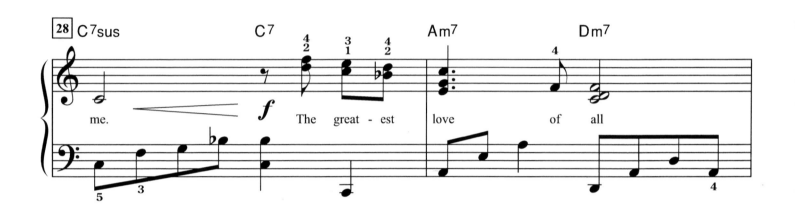

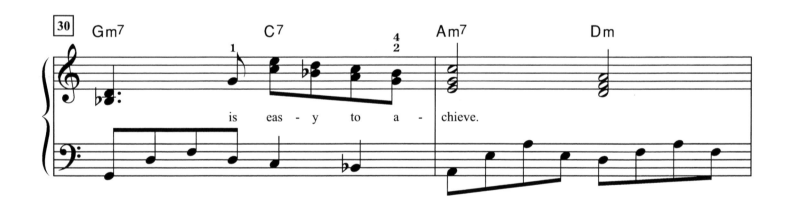

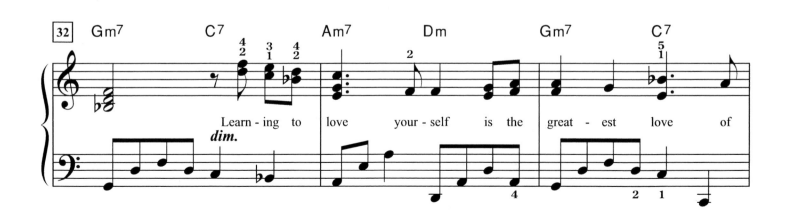

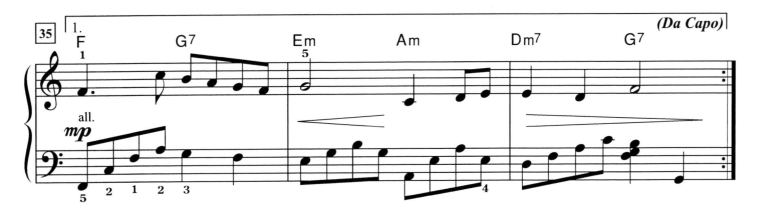

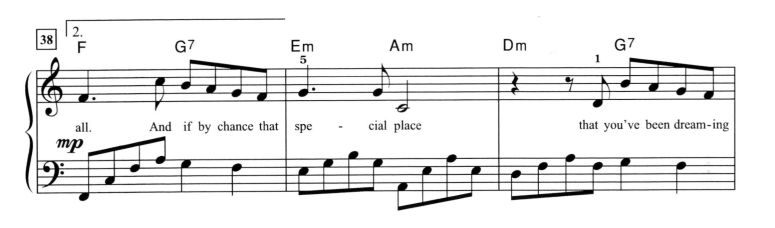

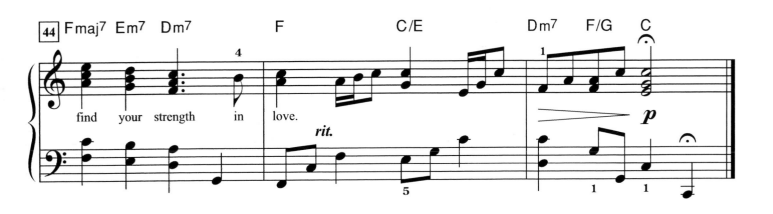

HEART

"Heart" is from the musical comedy *Damn Yankees*, which opened on Broadway in 1955. The plot is based on *Faust* but is set in 1950s Washington, D.C. "Heart" is sung by members of the Washington Senators—the jinxed baseball team which receives help from Joe Boyd, who sells his soul to the devil to become the "long ball hitter the Senators need." Richard Adler and Jerry Ross, the writers of *Damn Yankees*, also collaborated on the Broadway hit *The Pajama Game*. Sadly, Jerry Ross died just months after *Damn Yankees* opened.

Words and Music by Richard Adler and Jerry Ross
Arranged by Dan Coates

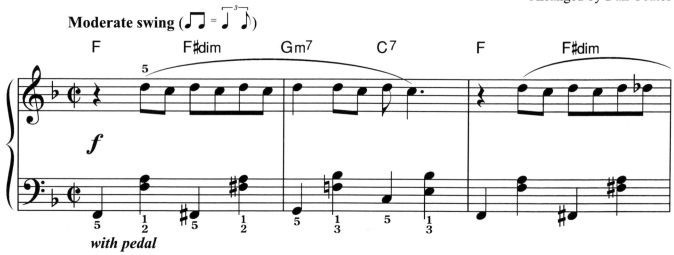

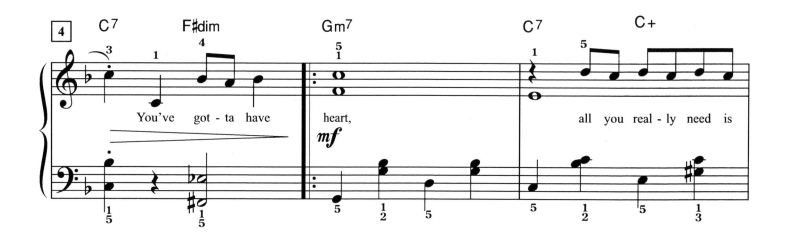

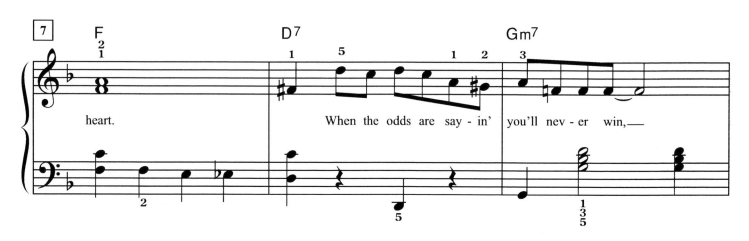

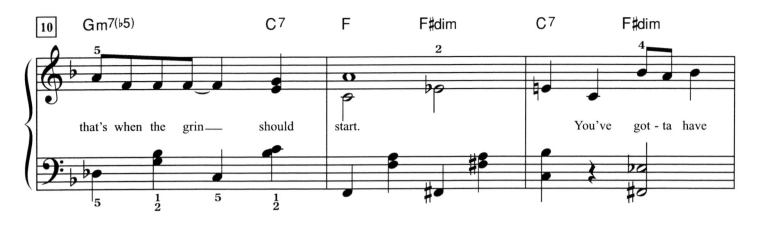

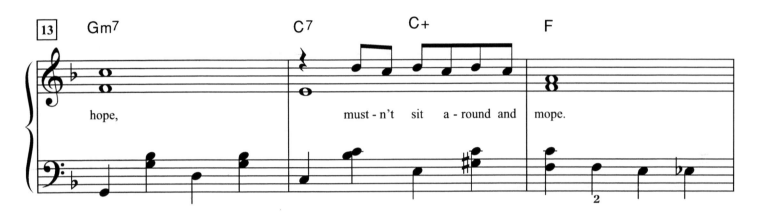

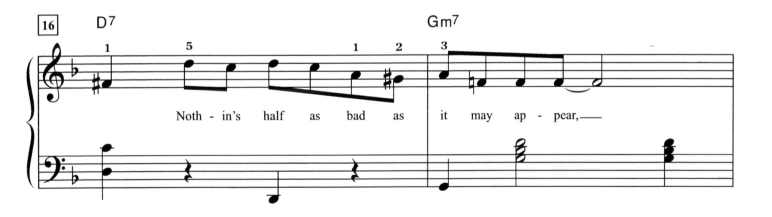

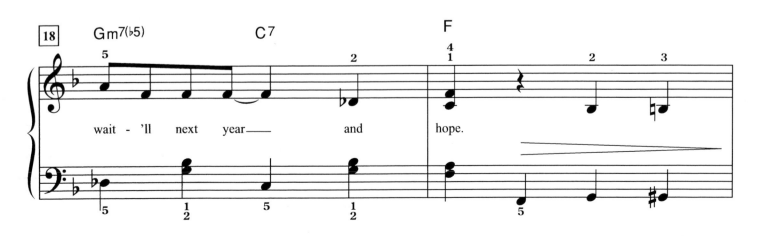

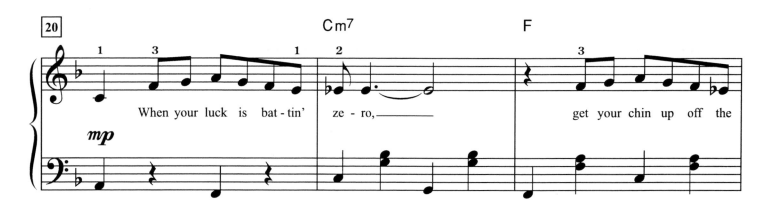

When your luck is bat-tin' ze-ro,_____ get your chin up off the

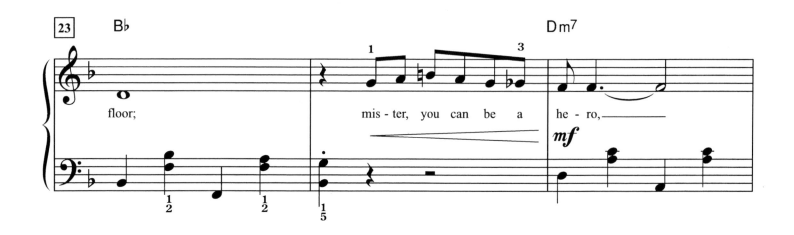

floor; mis-ter, you can be a he-ro,_____

you can o-pen an-y door, there's noth-in' to it but to do it. You've got-ta have

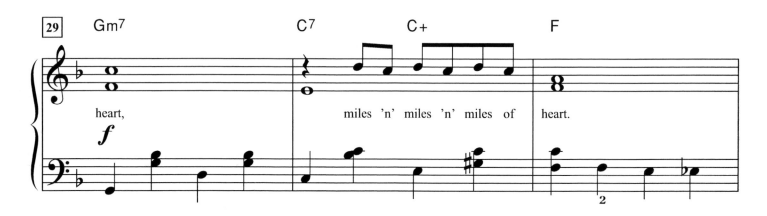

heart, miles 'n' miles 'n' miles of heart.

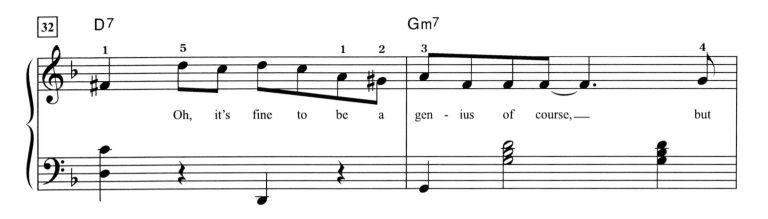

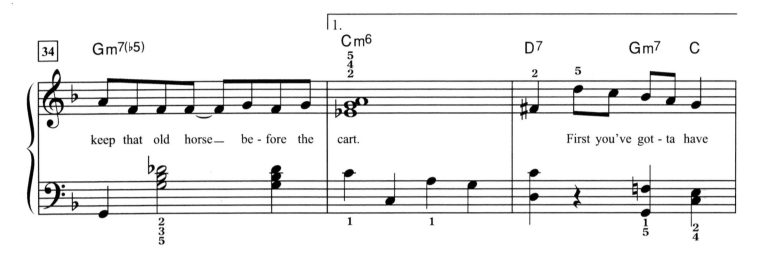

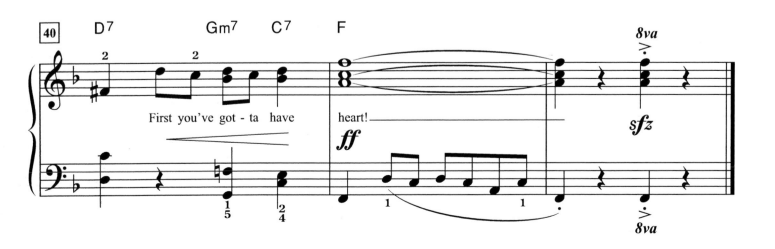

HEDWIG'S THEME
(FROM *HARRY POTTER AND THE SORCERER'S STONE*)

British author J. K. Rowling's *Harry Potter* fantasy novels have sold over 400 million copies worldwide, due in part to their transformation into series of blockbuster movies. John Williams composed "Hedwig's Theme" for *Harry Potter and the Sorcerer's Stone*, the first installment in the series, and the theme has been used in each film since.

By **JOHN WILLIAMS**
Arranged by Dan Coates

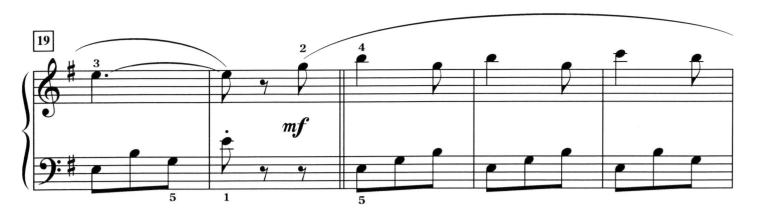

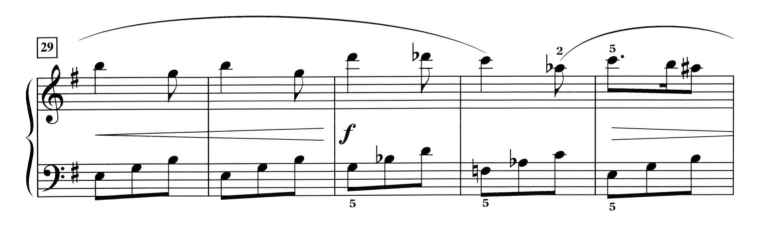

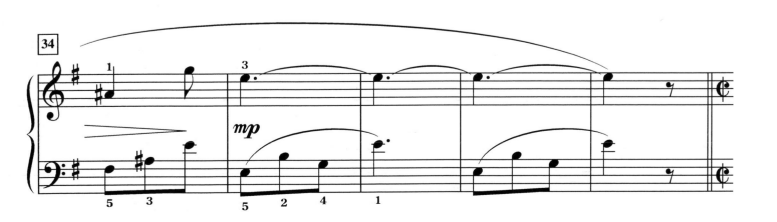

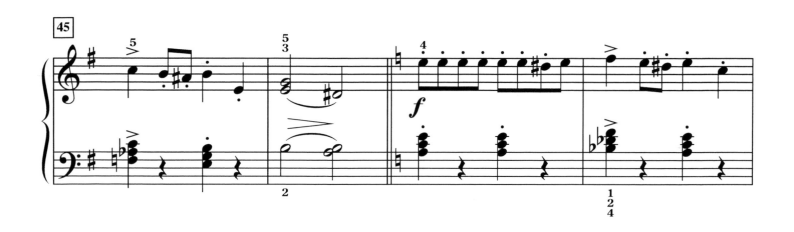

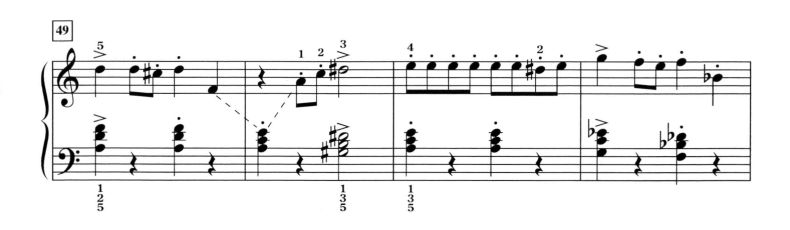

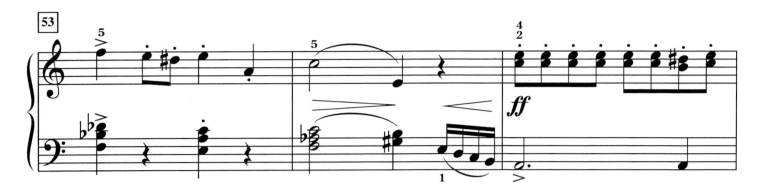

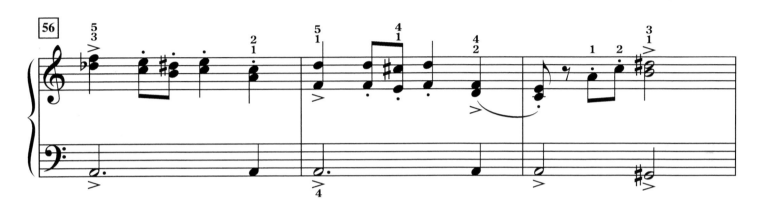

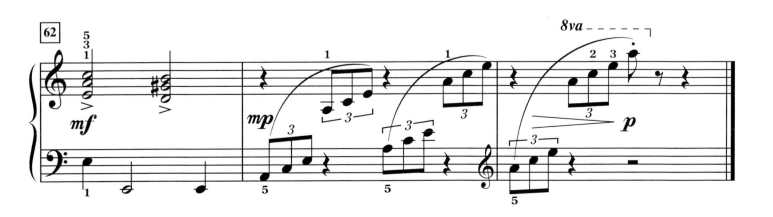

HEY THERE

"Hey There" is from the musical *The Pajama Game*, first published in 1954. The original Broadway production is credited with kick-starting the career of Shirley MacLaine. Director and producer Hal B. Wallis was an audience member at one of MacLaine's performances and signed her to Paramount Pictures. Rosemary Clooney and Sammy Davis Jr. both had #1 hits on the pop charts with their versions of "Hey There." The 2006 revival of *The Pajama Game* starred Harry Connick Jr.

Words and Music by Richard Adler and Jerry Ross
Arranged by Dan Coates

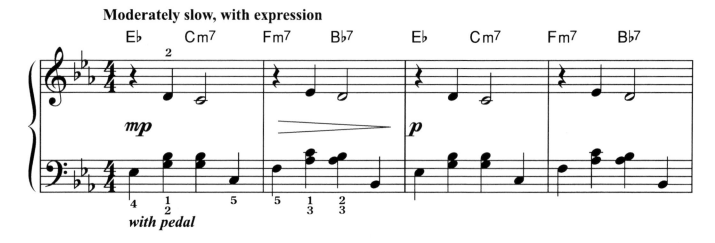

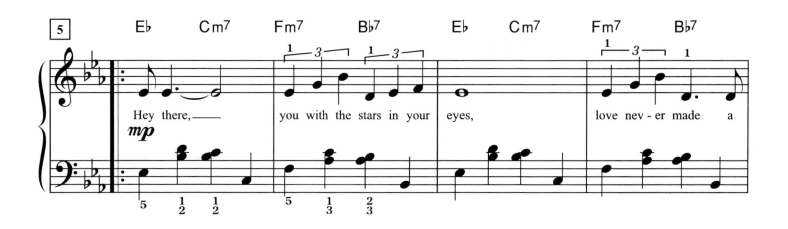

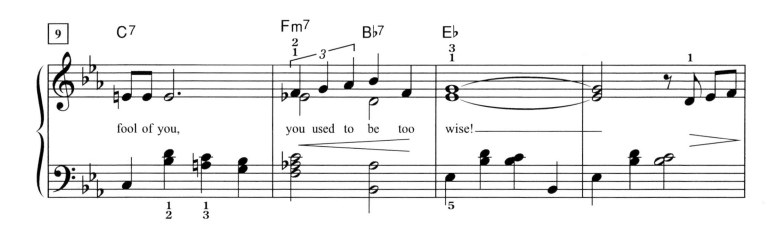

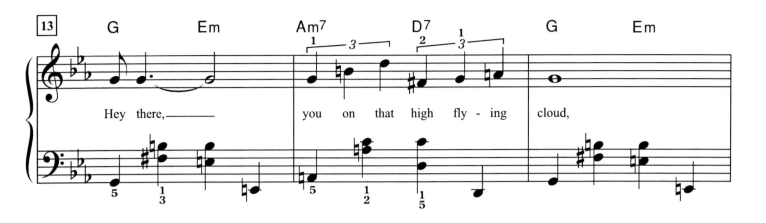

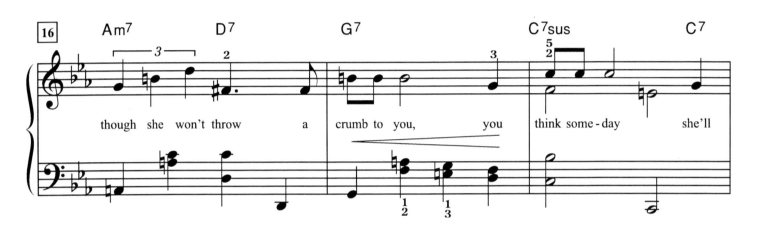

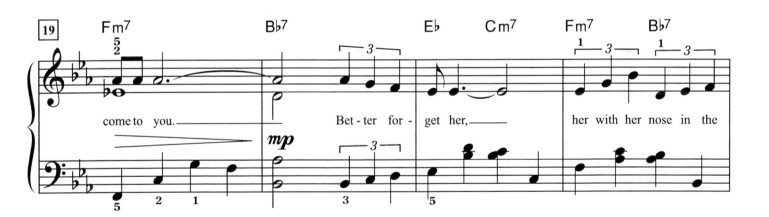

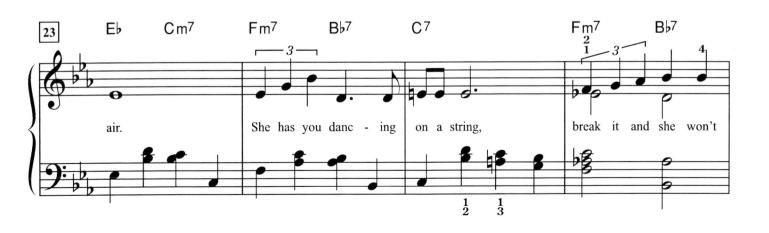

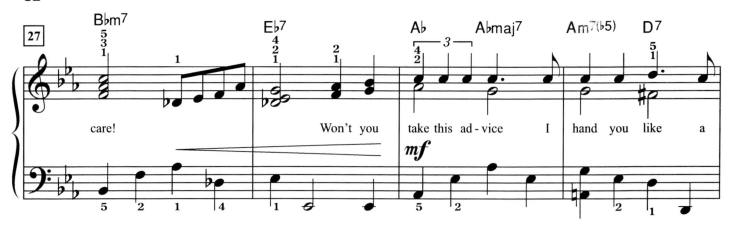

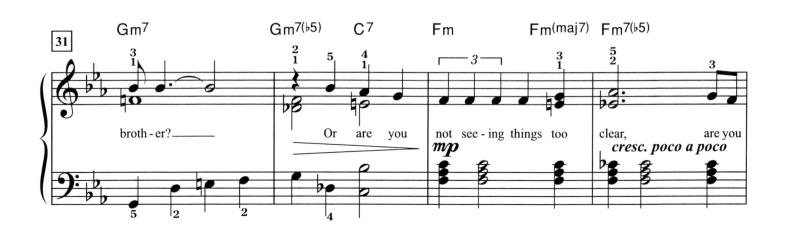

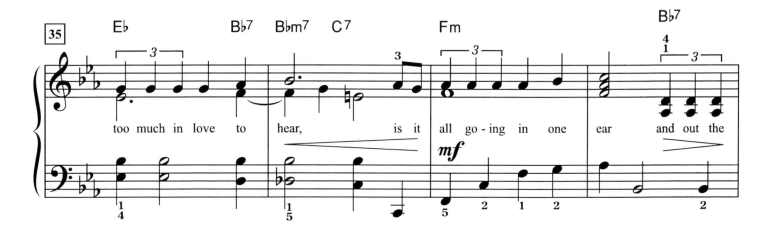

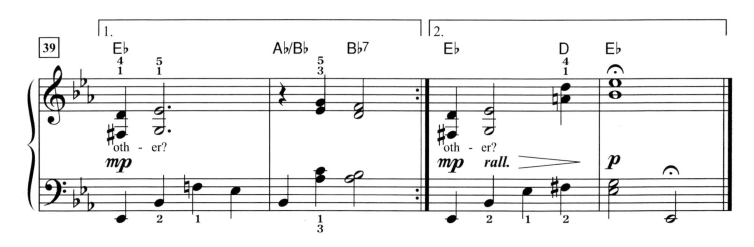

HEY THERE DELILAH

While "Hey There Delilah" was the third single from Plain White T's 2005 album *All That We Needed*, it was their first huge hit and reached No. 1 on the Billboard Hot 100 in July of 2007. Their follow-up album, *Every Second Counts*, offered a bonus track of "Hey There Delilah" with a string section.

Words and Music by Tom Higgenson
Arranged by Dan Coates

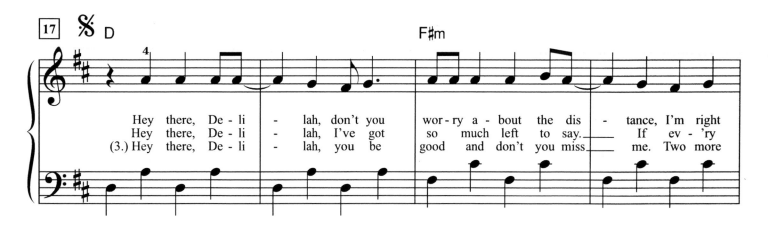

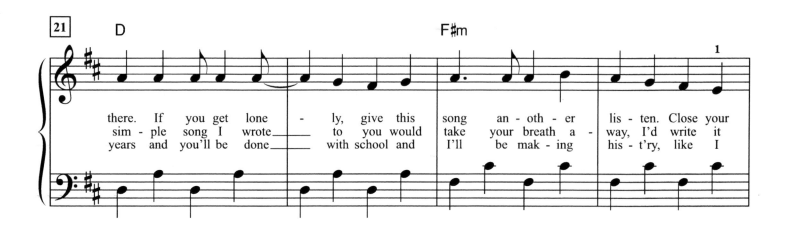

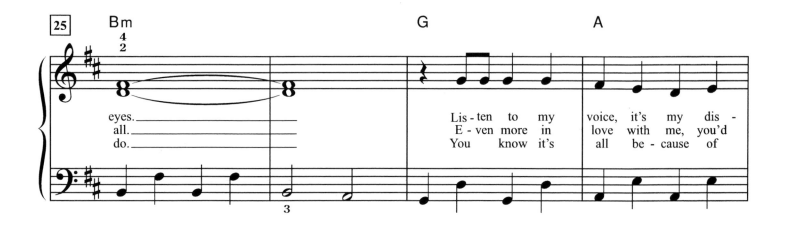

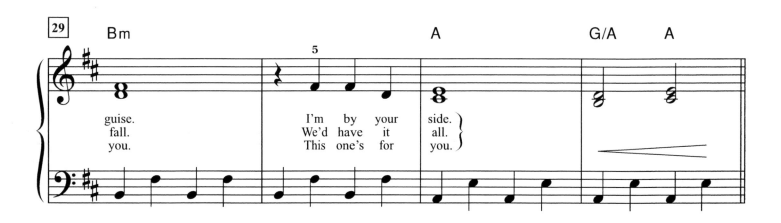

HOLD ME, THRILL ME, KISS ME

"Hold Me, Thrill Me, Kiss Me" was a hit pop song in two decades. The original version, recorded by Karen Chandler, stayed on the pop charts for 18 weeks in October of 1952. In 1965, the recording by Mel Carter, which is also the version that is more often heard, peaked at #8. Most recently, Clay Aiken sang the classic when he was a contestant on American Idol.

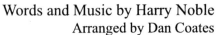

Words and Music by Harry Noble
Arranged by Dan Coates

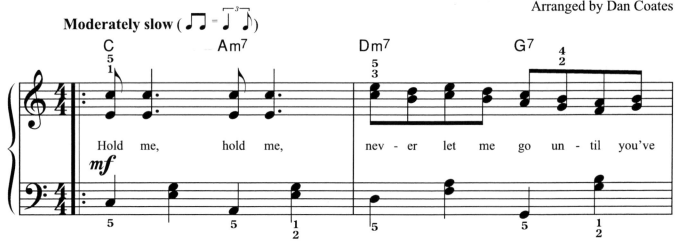

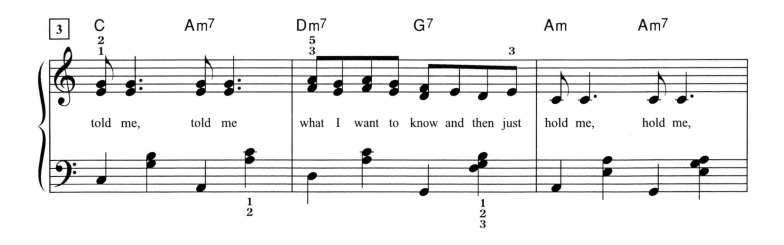

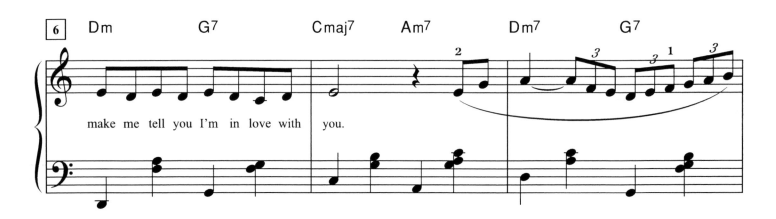

Thrill me, thrill me, walk me down the lane where shad-ows will be, will be

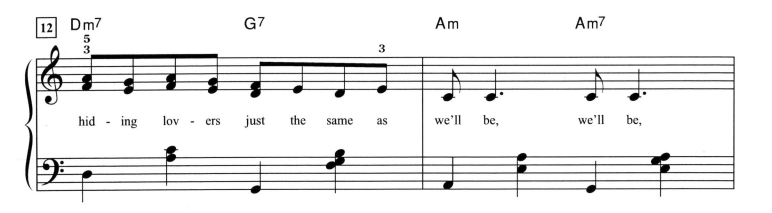

hid - ing lov - ers just the same as we'll be, we'll be,

when you make me tell you I love you. They

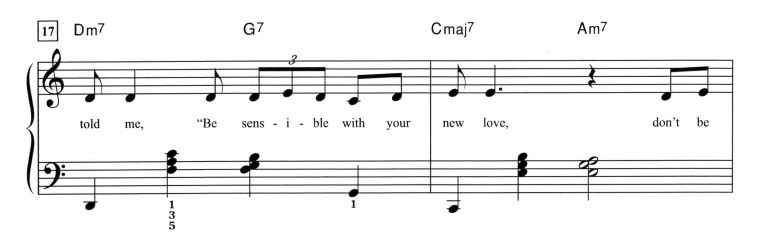

told me, "Be sens - i - ble with your new love, don't be

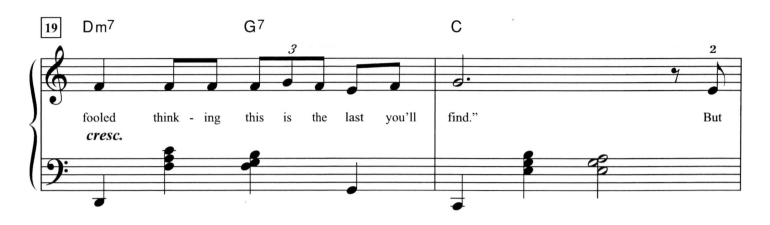

fooled think - ing this is the last you'll find." But

they nev - er stood in the dark with you, love, ———— when you

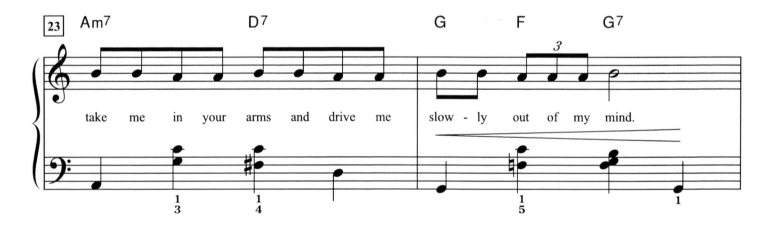

take me in your arms and drive me slow - ly out of my mind.

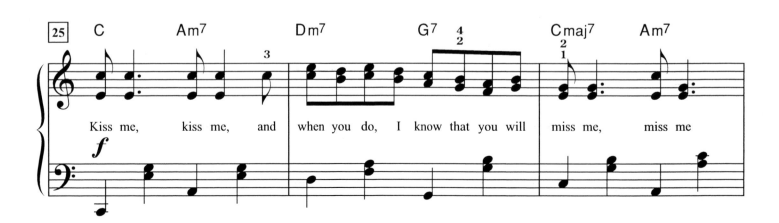

Kiss me, kiss me, and when you do, I know that you will miss me, miss me

if we ev-er say a-dieu, so kiss me, kiss me, make me tell you I'm in love with

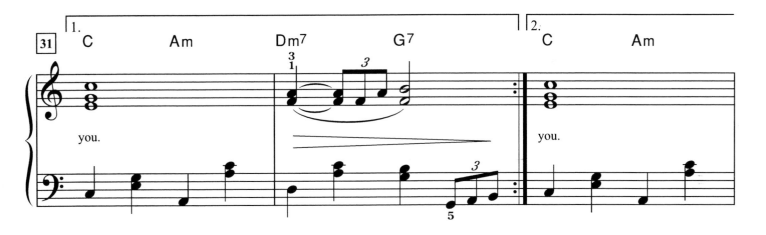

you. you.

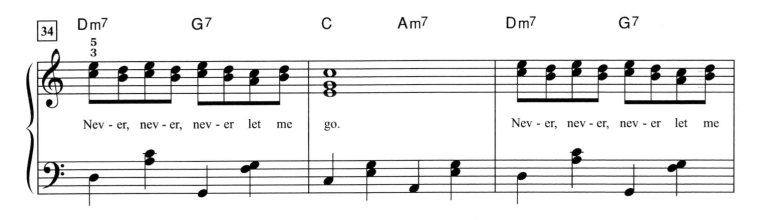

Nev-er, nev-er, nev-er let me go. Nev-er, nev-er, nev-er let me

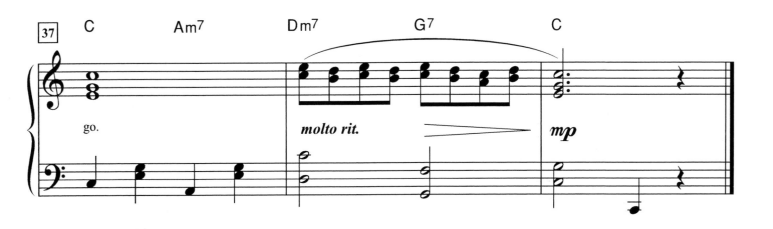

go. *molto rit.* *mp*

HOME

Featured on Michael Bublé's second album, *It's Time* (2005), "Home" was written by Bublé, Alan Chang (his music director), and Amy Foster (producer David Foster's daughter). The song topped the charts in both Canada and the U. S., crossing over from the adult contemporary to the pop charts. In 2008, country artist Blake Shelton's version of "Home" reached the top of the Billboard Hot Country Songs chart.

Words and Music by
Michael Bublé, Alan Chang and Amy Foster
Arranged by Dan Coates

HOTEL CALIFORNIA

Hotel California was released by the Eagles in 1976 and was the first Eagles album without founding member Bernie Leadon. Since then it has sold over 16 million copies in the U.S. alone. The album was #1 on the Billboard 200 for eight weeks in 1977 and has become one of the top 15 best-selling albums of all time in any category.

Words and Music by Don Henley,
Glenn Frey, and Don Felder
Arranged by Dan Coates

Moderate rock beat

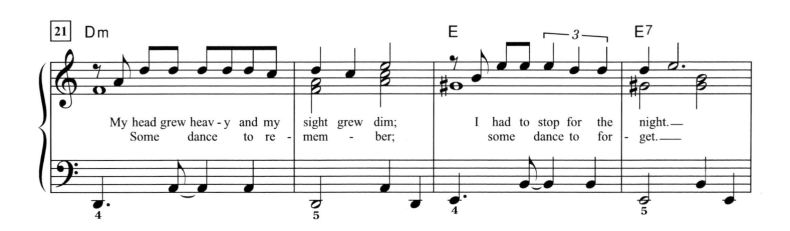

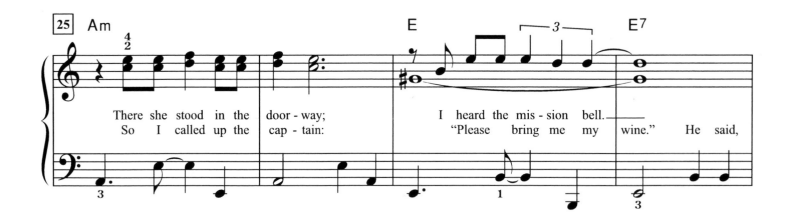

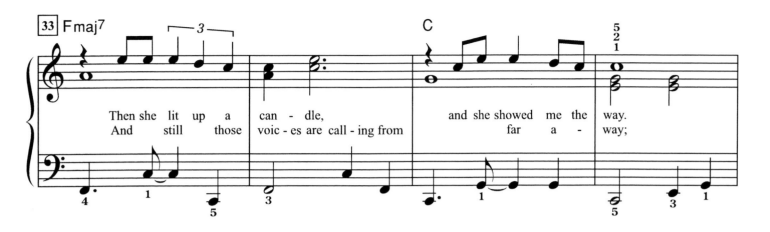

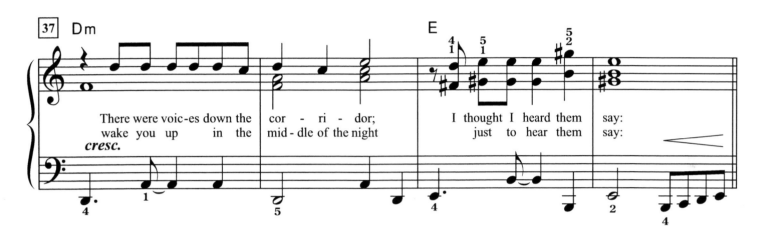

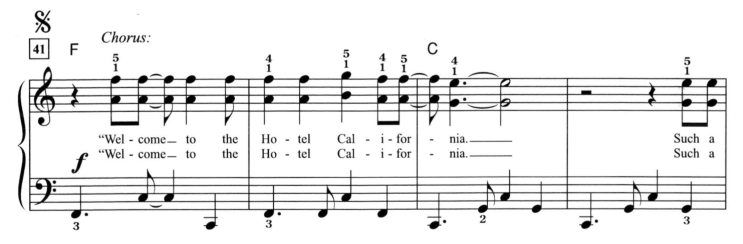

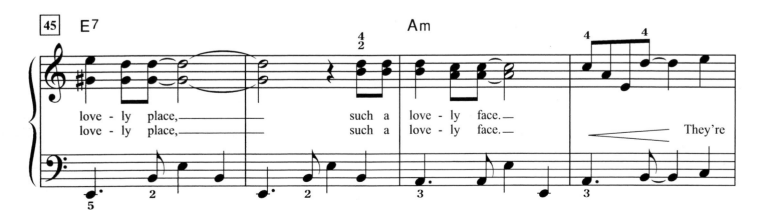

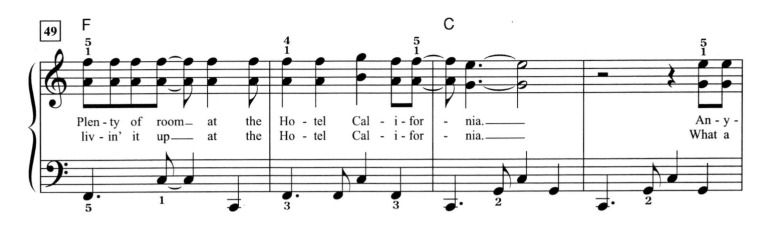

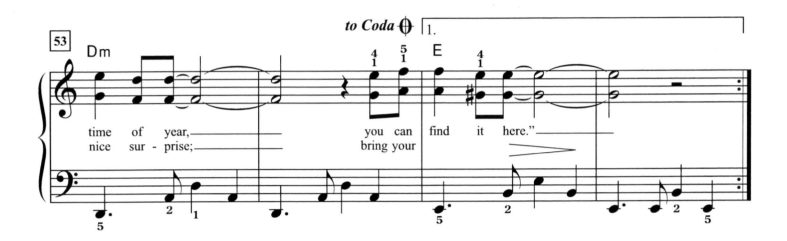

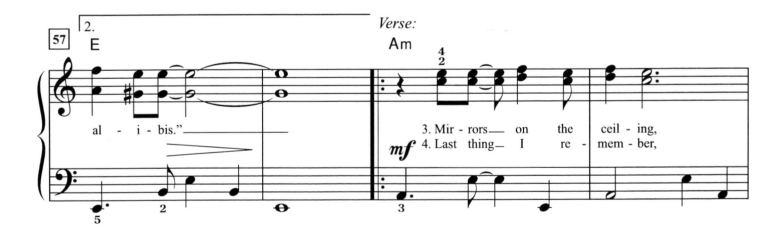

pris - on - ers here
pas - sage back to the

of our own— de -vice.”
place I was— be -fore.

And in the mas - ter’s—
“Re - lax,” said the

cham - bers,
night man.

they gath - ered for the feast.
“We are pro - grammed to re - ceive.

They stab it— with their
You can check out— an - y

1.

2.

D.S. al Coda

steel - y knives, but they
time you like, but

just can’t— kill the beast.
you can— nev - er

leave.”

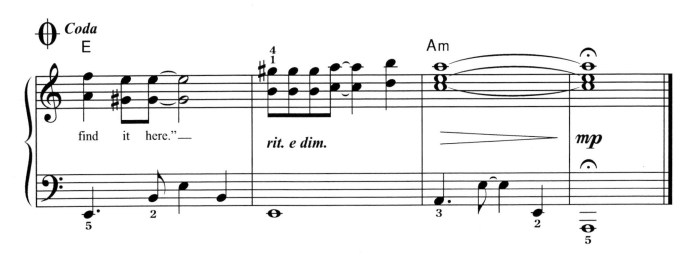

Coda

find it here.”—

rit. e dim.

mp

HOW DEEP IS YOUR LOVE

The Bee Gees recorded "How Deep Is Your Love" in 1977, and soon after the song rose to the top of the Billboard Charts staying in the top 10 for 17 weeks. It was used along with their other huge hit, "Stayin' Alive," in *Saturday Night Fever,* the John Travolta film that helped popularize disco music around the world.

Words and Music by Barry Gibb,
Maurice Gibb and Robin Gibb
Arranged by Dan Coates

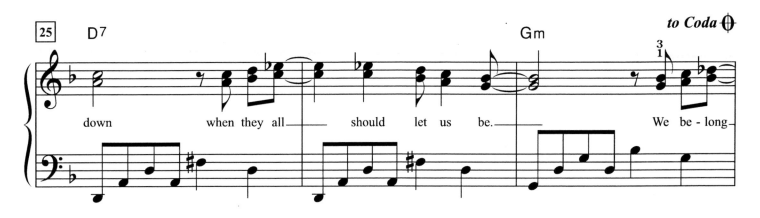

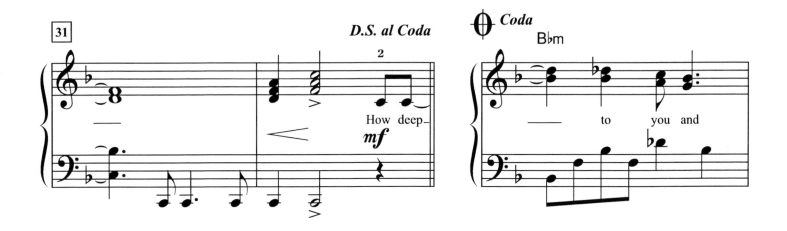

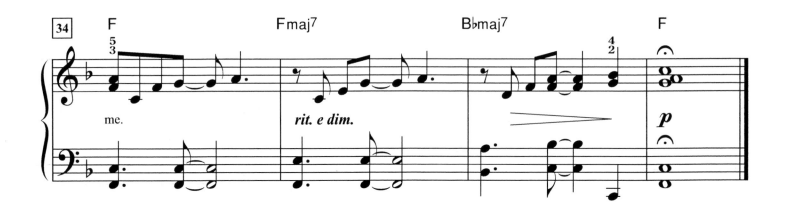

I COULD HAVE DANCED ALL NIGHT

"I Could Have Danced All Night" was first performed by Julie Andrews (in the role of Eliza Doolittle) in the original Broadway production of *My Fair Lady*. Doolittle is moved to sing after an unexpected dance with her tutor, Henry Higgins. In the 1964 film, Audrey Hepburn played the role of Doolittle, but the song was sung by Marni Nixon and dubbed into the film.

Lyrics by Alan Jay Lerner
Music by Frederick Loewe
Arranged by Dan Coates

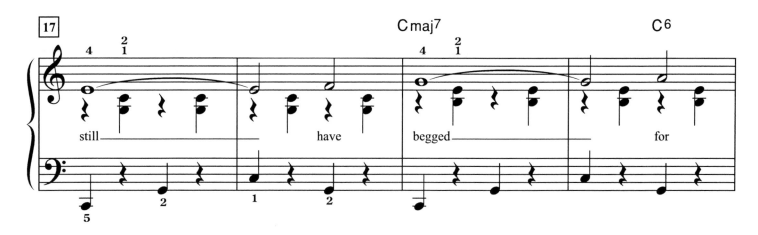

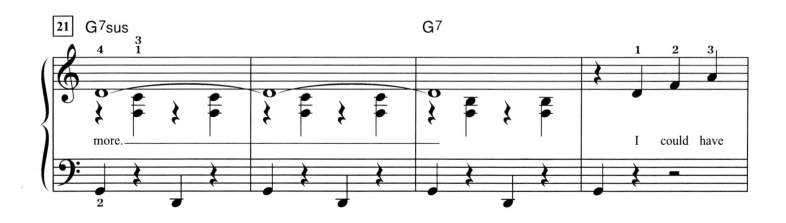

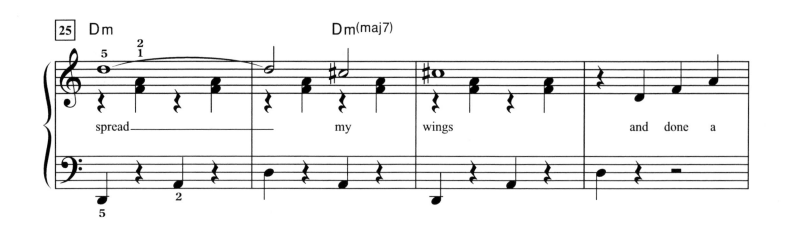

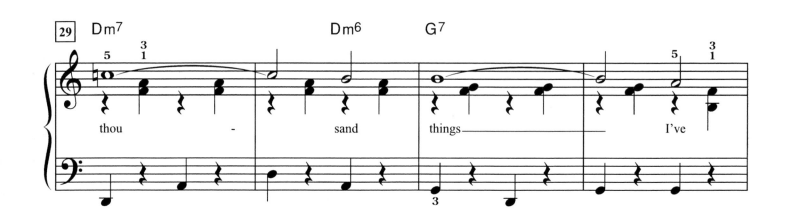

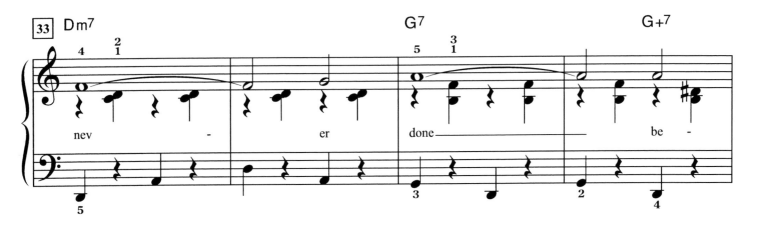

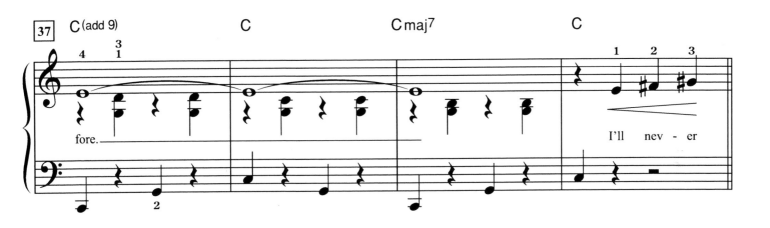

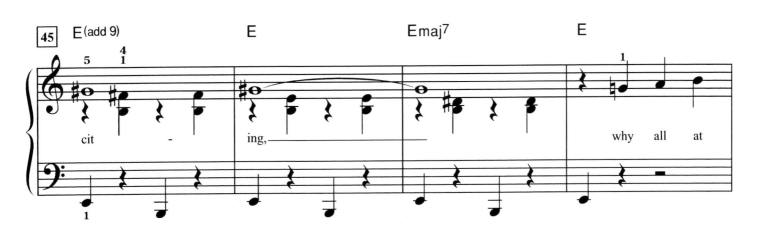

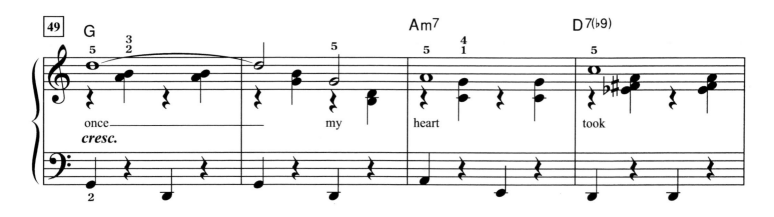

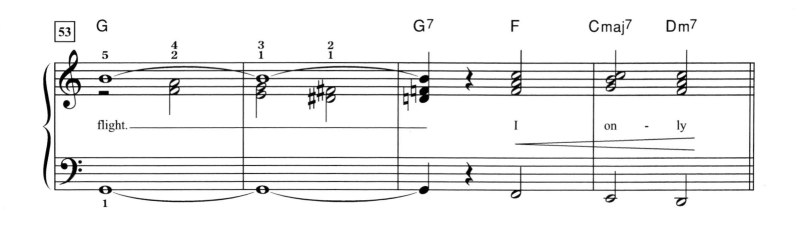

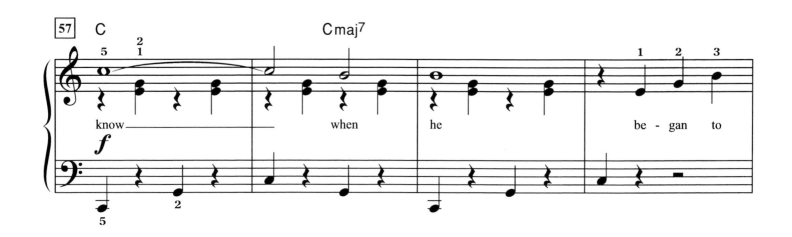

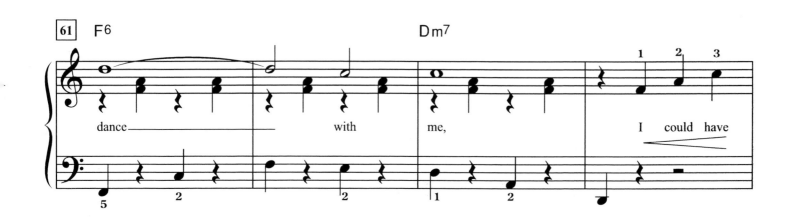

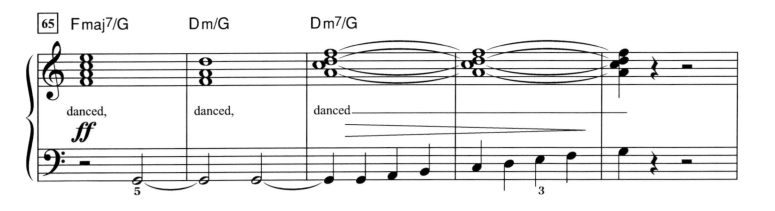

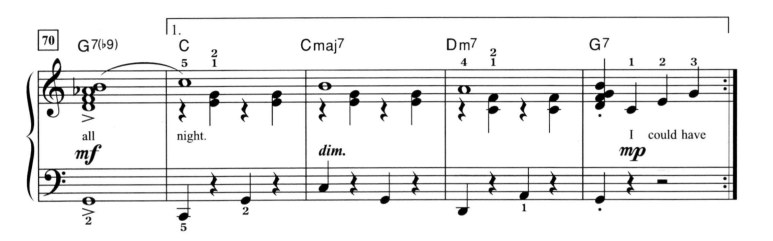

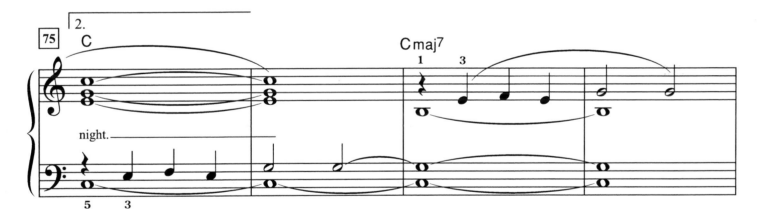

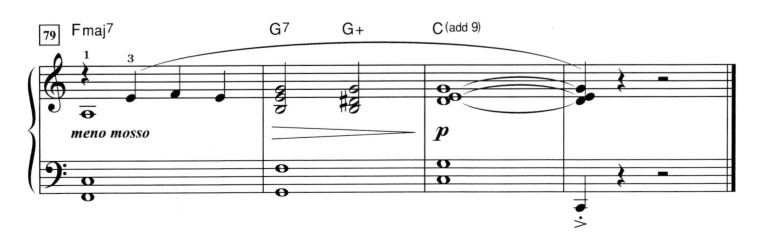

I DON'T WANT TO MISS A THING

Aerosmith recorded the power ballad "I Don't Want to Miss a Thing" in 1998 for the sci-fi blockbuster *Armageddon*. The single debuted on the Billboard Hot 100 at #1, was nominated for an Academy Award, and introduced the band to a new generation of listeners.

Words and Music by Diane Warren
Arranged by Dan Coates

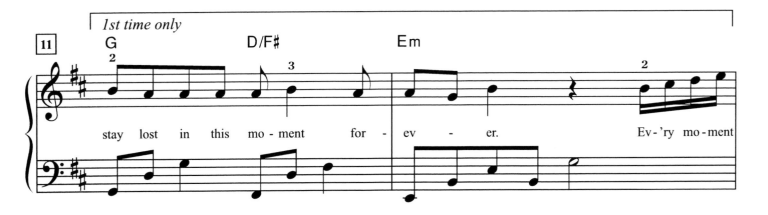

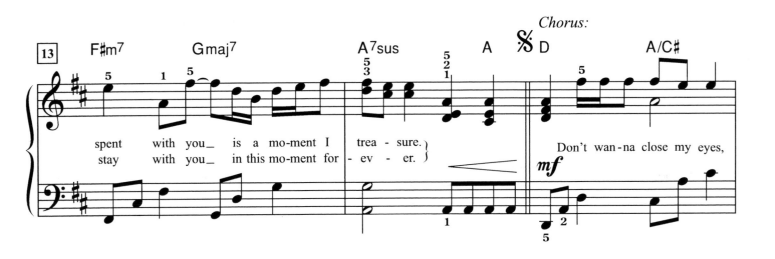

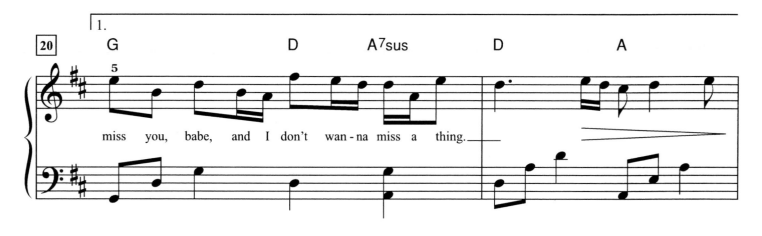

Bridge:

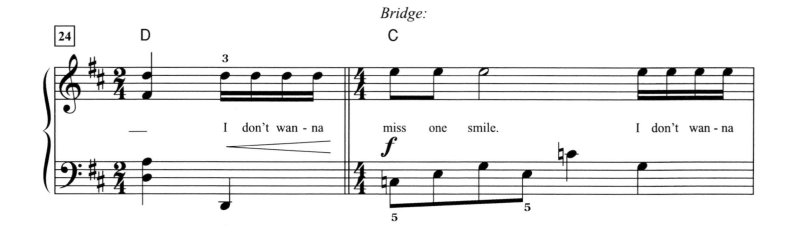

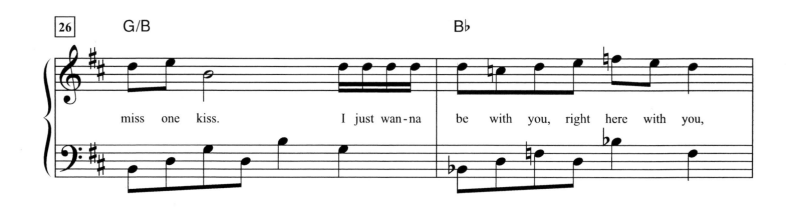

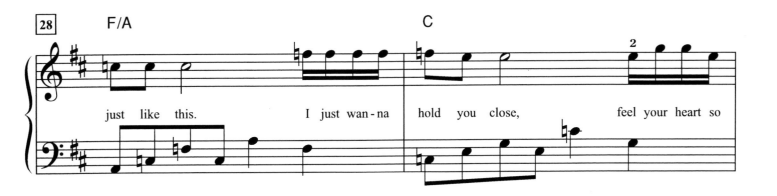

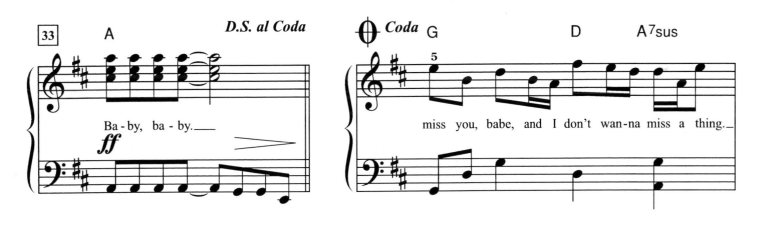

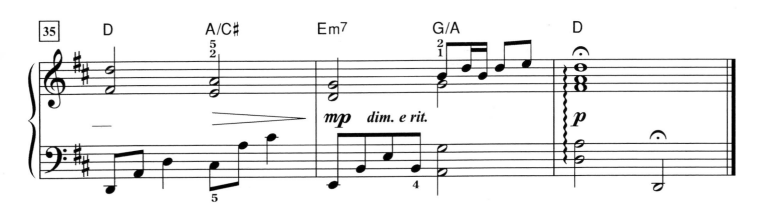

I GET A KICK OUT OF YOU

One of the hits from the musical *Anything Goes,* "I Get a Kick Out of You" was originally sung by Ethel Merman. Many other singers—from Frank Sinatra to Patti Lupone—have performed this song, often varying the lyrics. "I Get a Kick Out of You," through all of its variations, remains a lighthearted expression of affection in the Broadway style.

Words and Music by Cole Porter
Arranged by Dan Coates

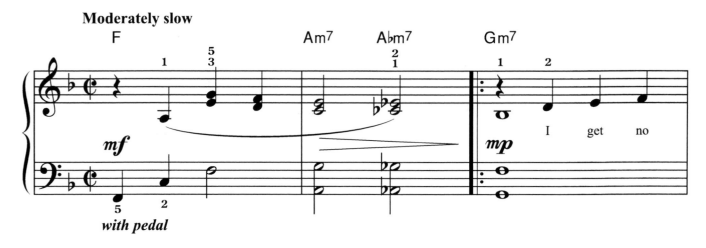

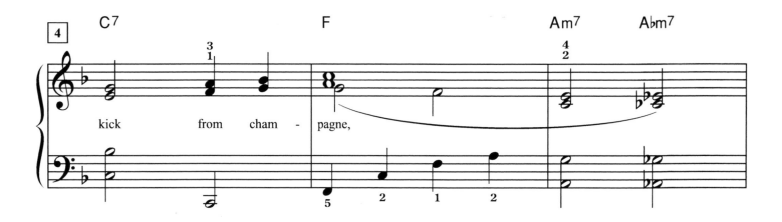

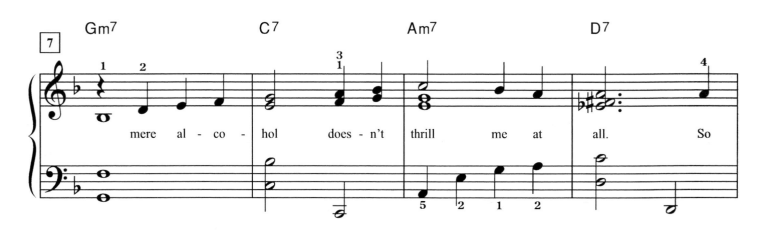

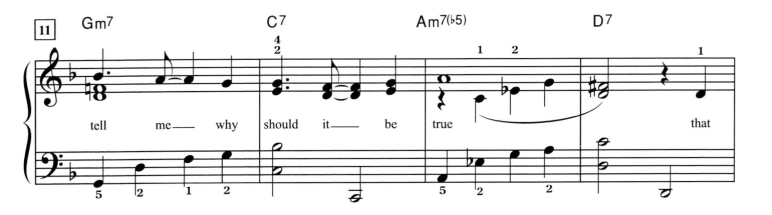

11 Gm7 — C7 — Am7(♭5) — D7

tell me — why should it — be true that

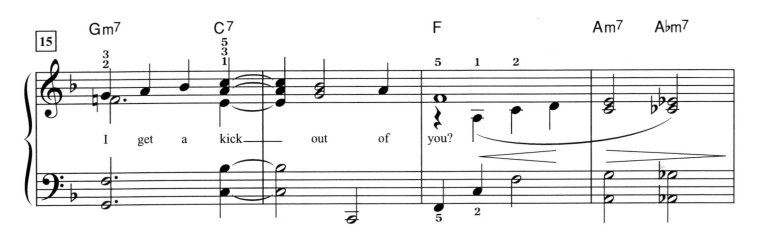

15 Gm7 — C7 — F — Am7 — A♭m7

I get a kick — out of you?

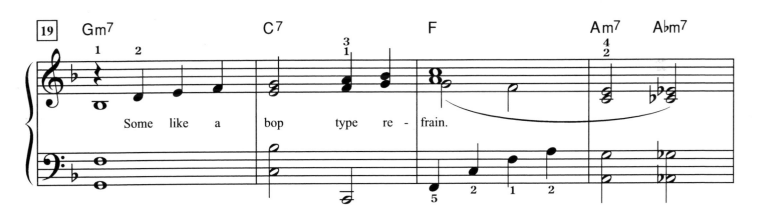

19 Gm7 — C7 — F — Am7 — A♭m7

Some like a bop type re - frain.

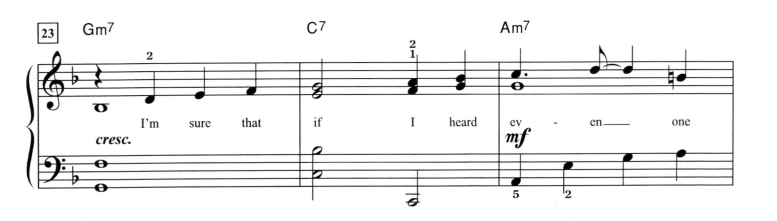

23 Gm7 — C7 — Am7

I'm sure that if I heard ev - en — one

cresc. *mf*

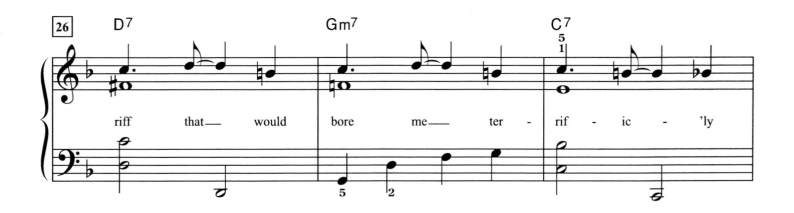

riff that— would bore me— ter - rif - ic - 'ly

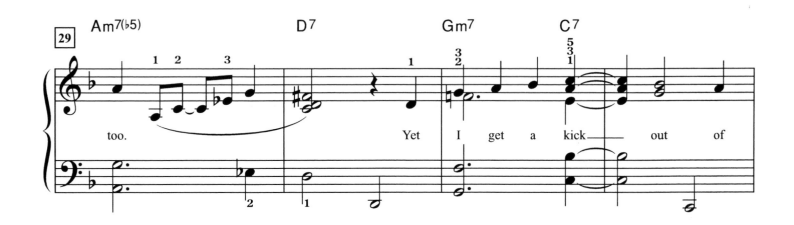

too. Yet I get a kick— out of

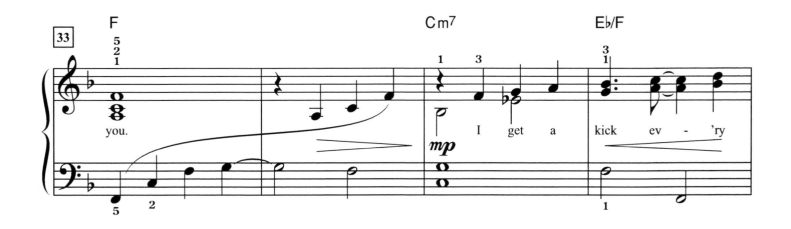

you. I get a kick ev - 'ry

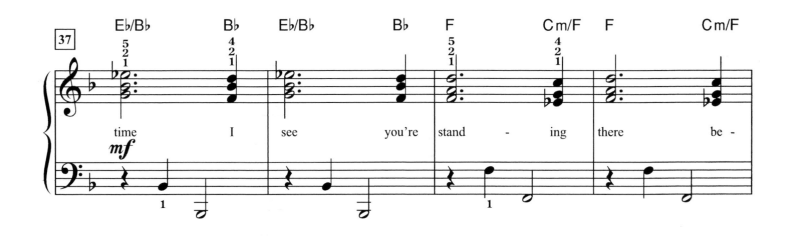

time I see you're stand - ing there be -

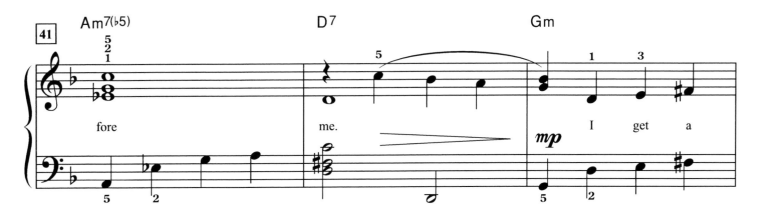

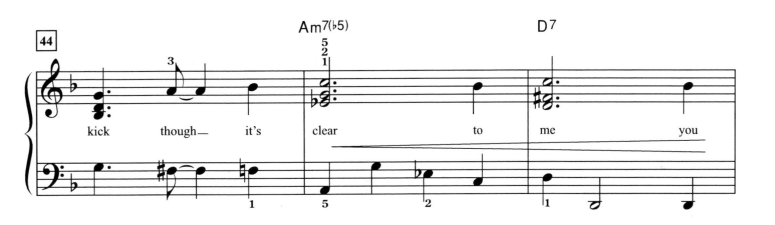

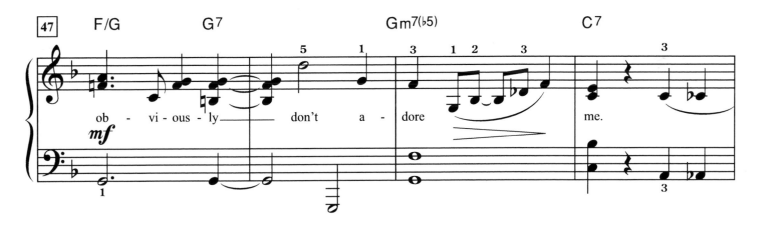

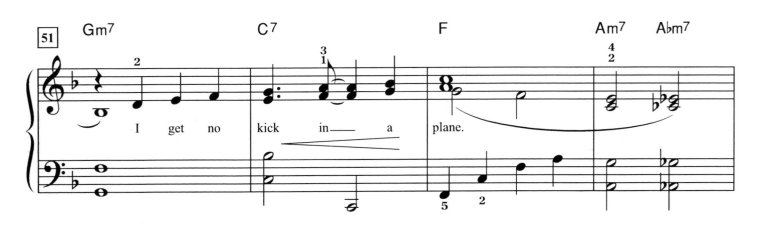

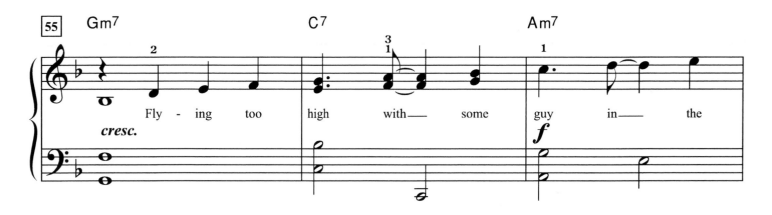

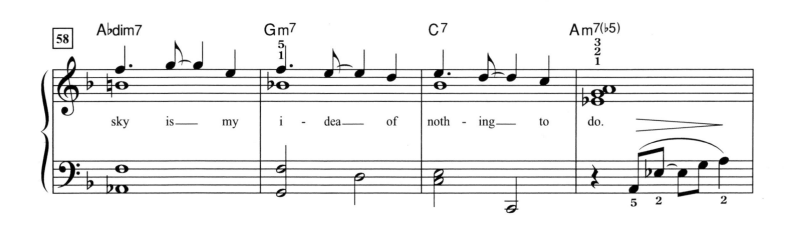

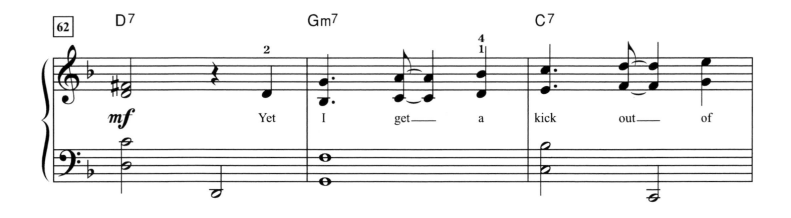

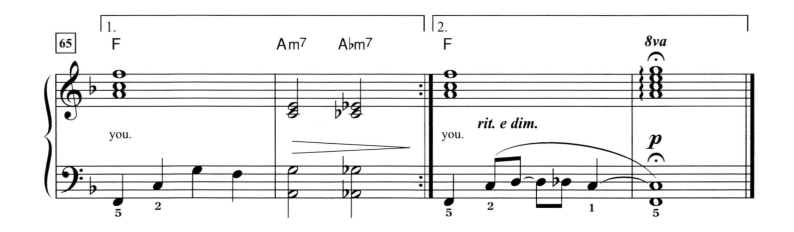

I GOT RHYTHM

Like so many jazz standards, "I Got Rhythm" originated in a musical. George and Ira Gershwin's *Girl Crazy* (1930) made stars of Ethel Merman and Judy Garland, and also introduced the world to many Gershwin classics including "But Not for Me," "Embraceable You," and "I Got Rhythm." In 1933, George Gershwin expanded "I Got Rhythm" into *Variations on "I Got Rhythm"* for piano and orchestra, which became his final classical concert piece. It was the only work he dedicated to his brother Ira.

Music and Lyrics by
George Gershwin and Ira Gershwin
Arranged by Dan Coates

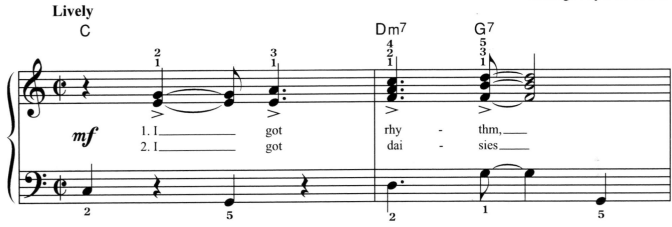

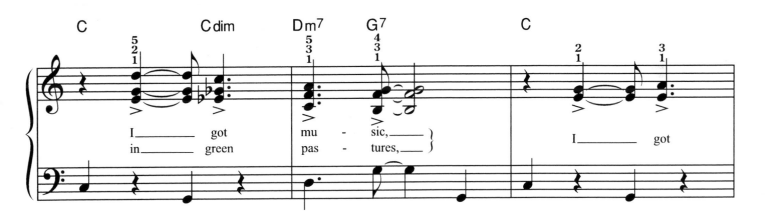

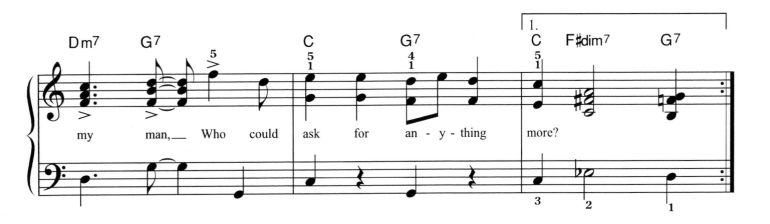

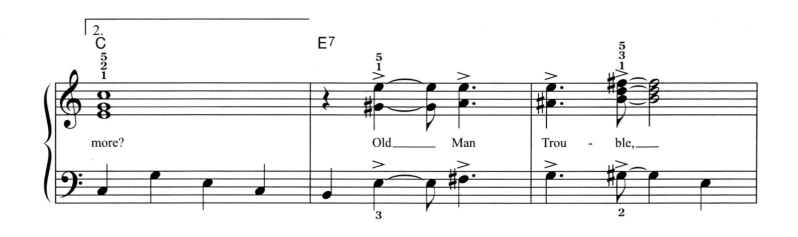

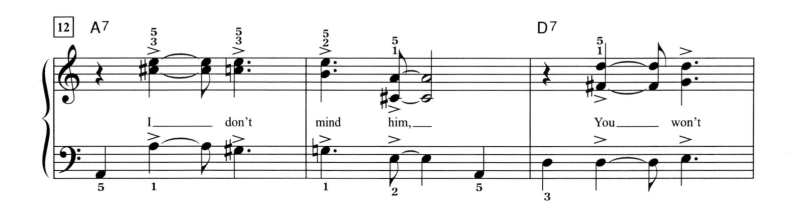

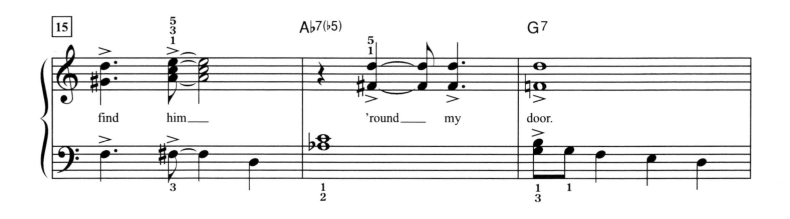

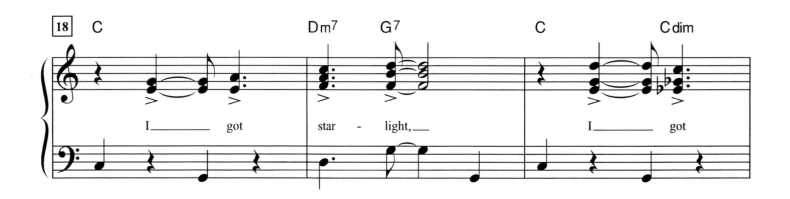

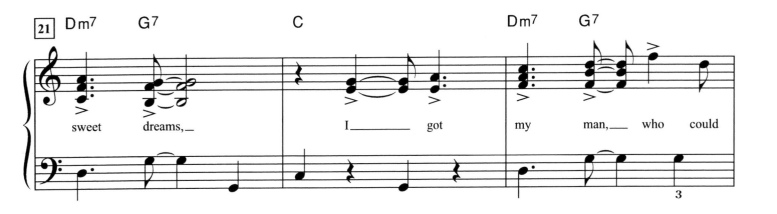

sweet dreams,___ I___ got my man,___ who could

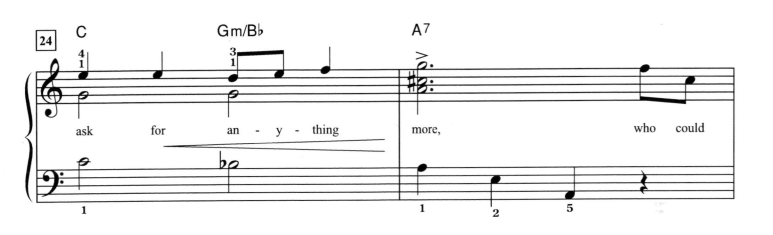

ask for an - y - thing more, who could

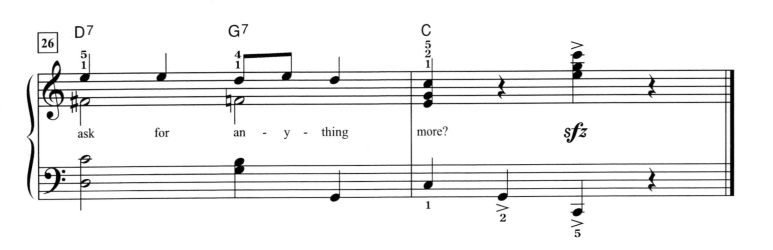

ask for an - y - thing more? *sfz*

I ONLY HAVE EYES FOR YOU

"I Only Have Eyes for You" is not only known as a standard but also as a 1950s pop song, made famous by The Flamingos. It was originally written for the 1934 musical film *Dames,* and in 1989 it won an ASCAP award for Most Performed Feature Film Standard. Many notable artists have recorded the song including Frank Sinatra, Peggy Lee and Art Garfunkel.

Words by Al Dubin
Music by Harry Warren
Arranged by Dan Coates

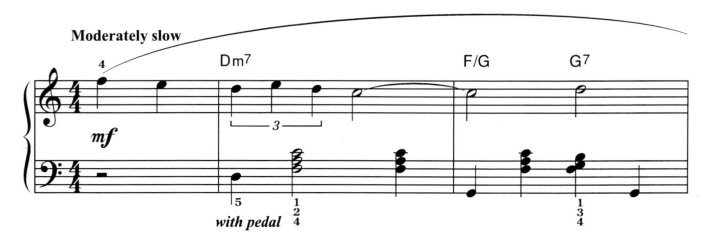

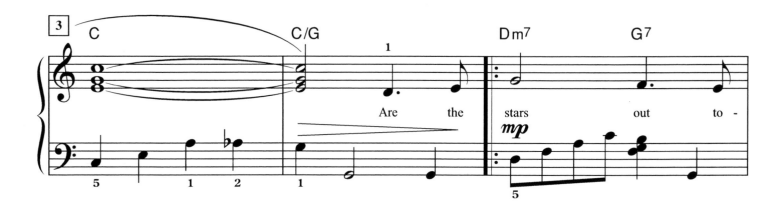

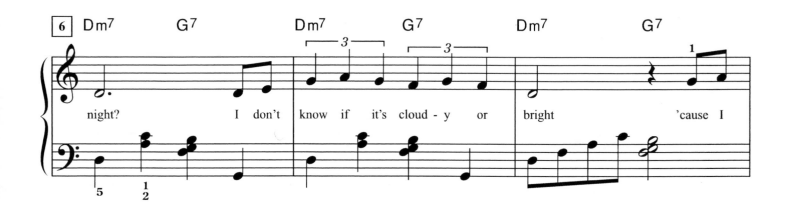

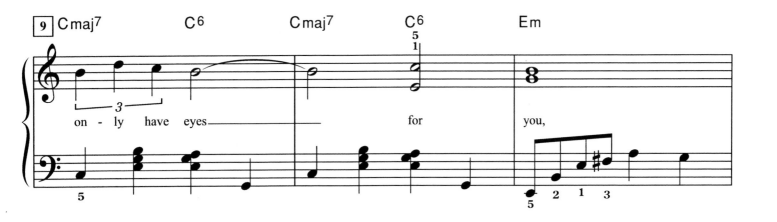

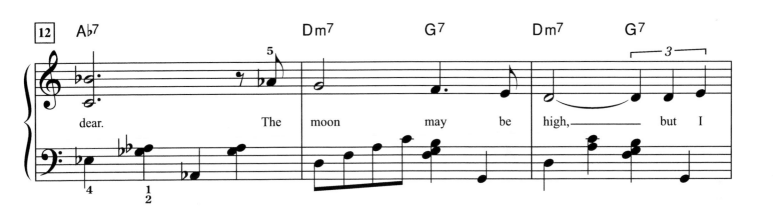

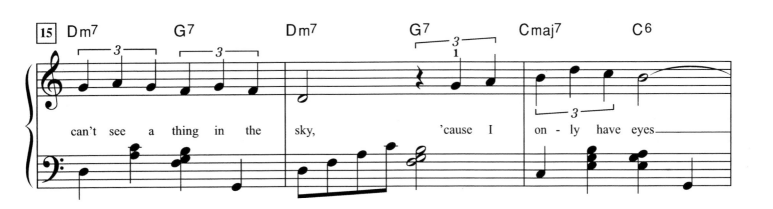

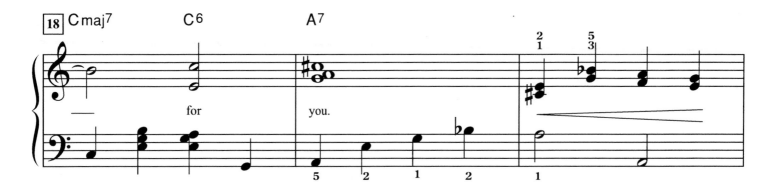

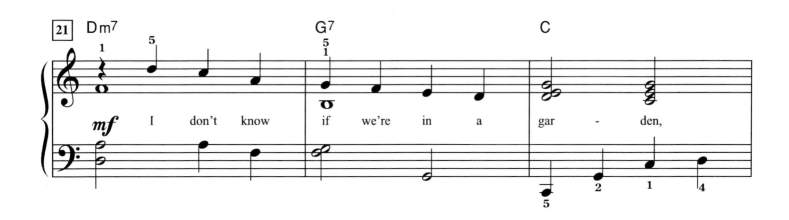

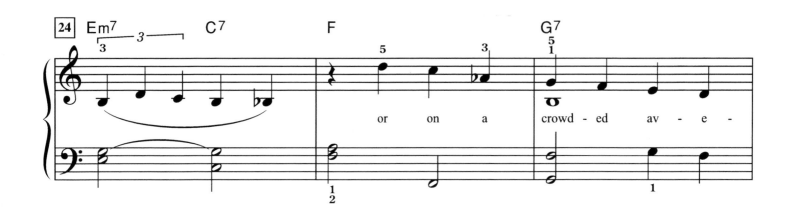

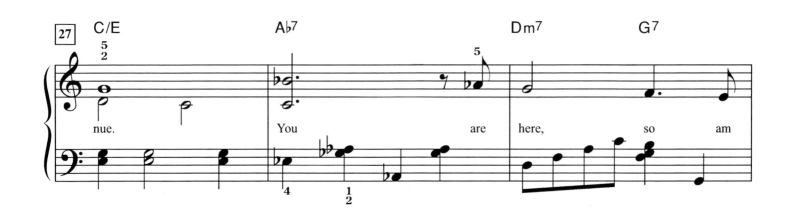

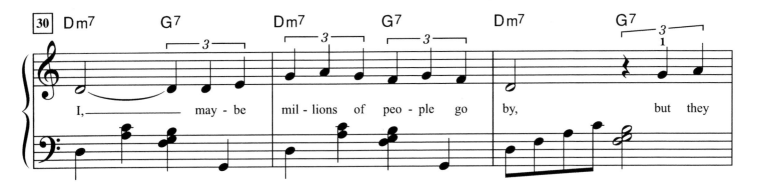

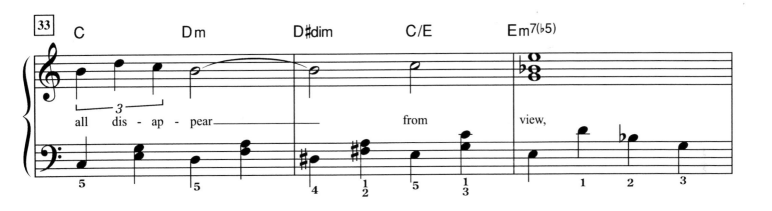

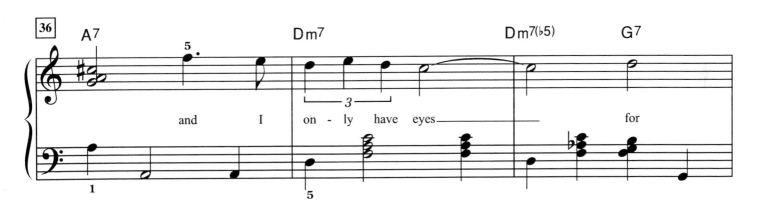

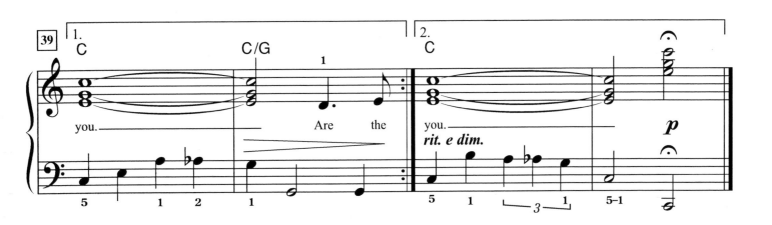

I SWEAR

"I Swear" was a big hit ballad for two acts in 1994. It was a #1 song on the U.S. Hot Country Songs chart for John Michael Montgomery and was included on his album *Kickin' It Up*. The R & B male vocal quartet All-4-One also recorded the song, releasing it on their self-titled debut album. Their version climbed to #1 on the Billboard Hot 100 and stayed there for 11 weeks.

Words and Music by
Gary Baker and Frank Myers
Arranged by Dan Coates

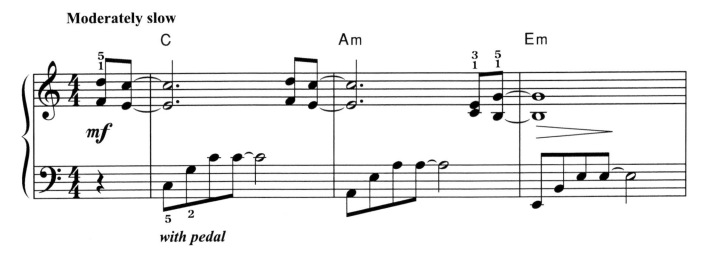

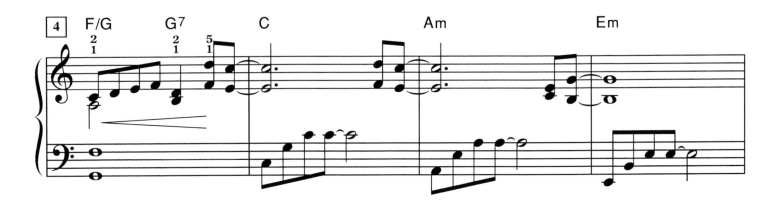

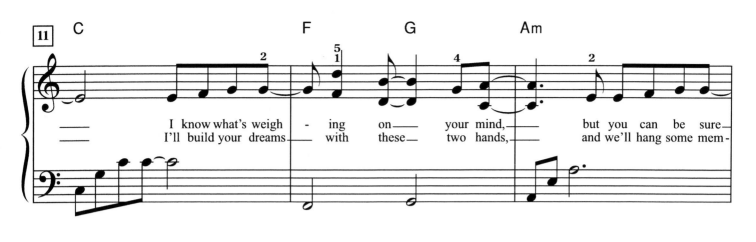

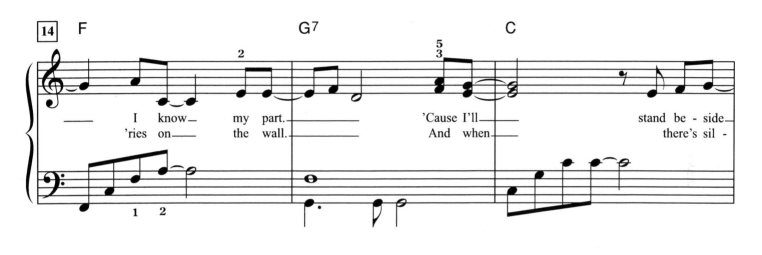

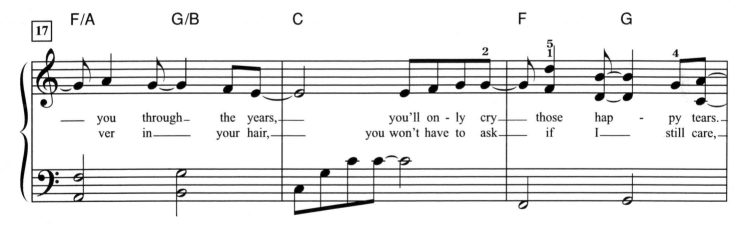

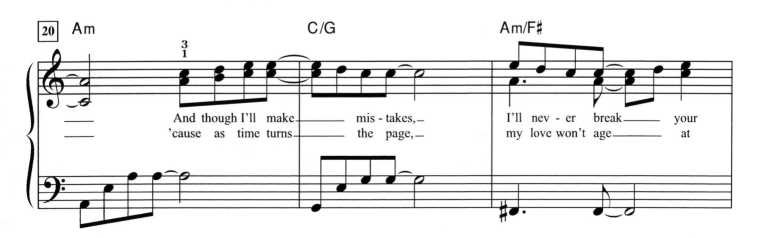

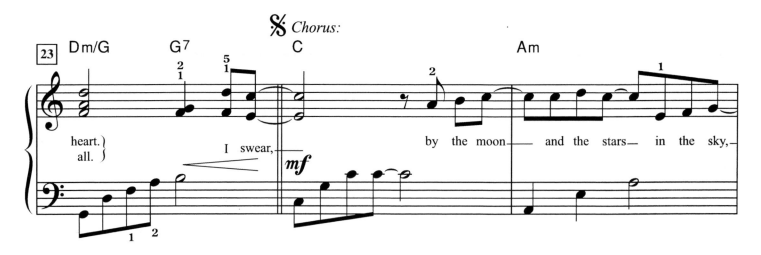

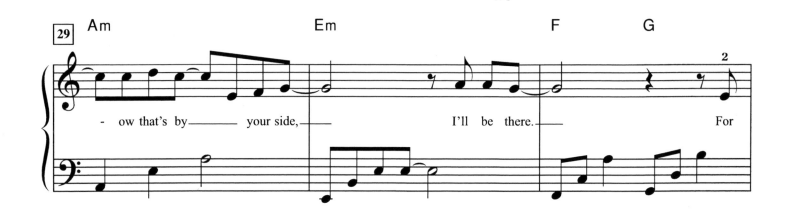

I'M IN THE MOOD FOR LOVE

"I'm in the Mood for Love" was first sung by Frances Langford in her film debut, *Every Night at Eight* (1935). She would star in many other films and would also perform regularly on U.S.O. tours during World War II. "I'm in the Mood for Love" became her signature song. Years later, it would also become the signature song for the character Alfalfa on the popular television series *Our Gang* (a.k.a. *The Little Rascals*).

Words and Music by
Jimmy McHugh and Dorothy Fields
Arranged by Dan Coates

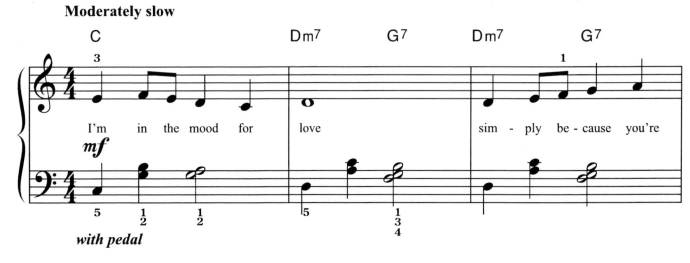

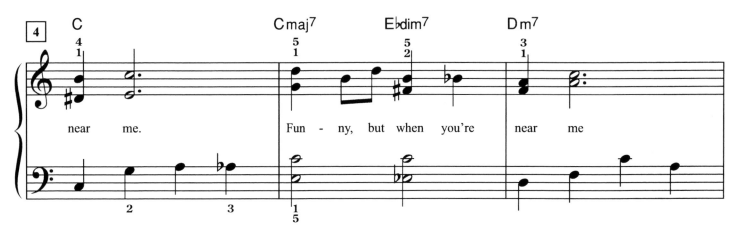

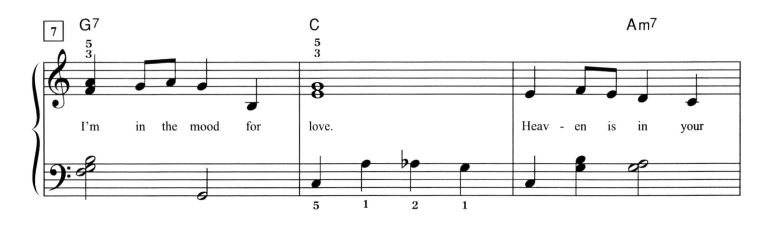

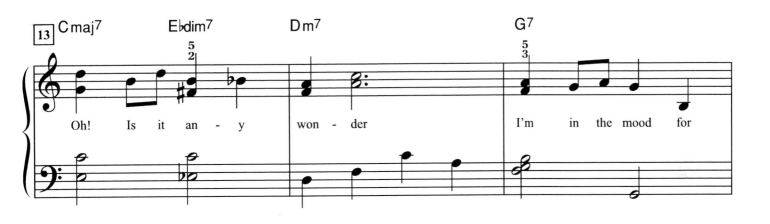

geth - er; now we are one, I'm not a - fraid!

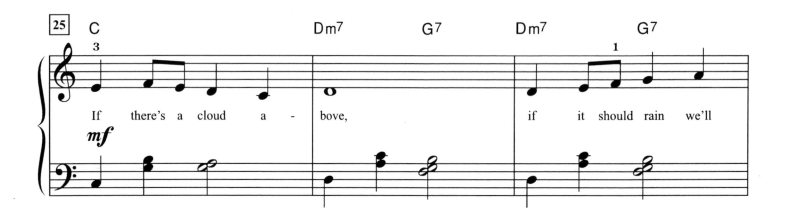

If there's a cloud a - bove, if it should rain we'll

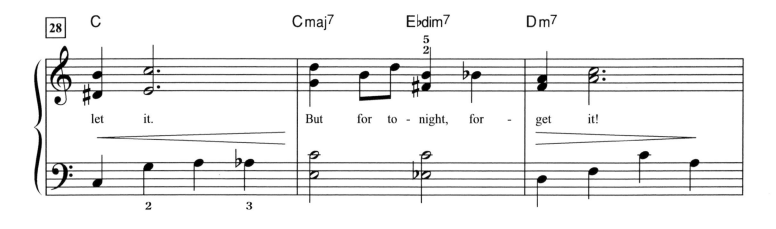

let it. But for to - night, for - get it!

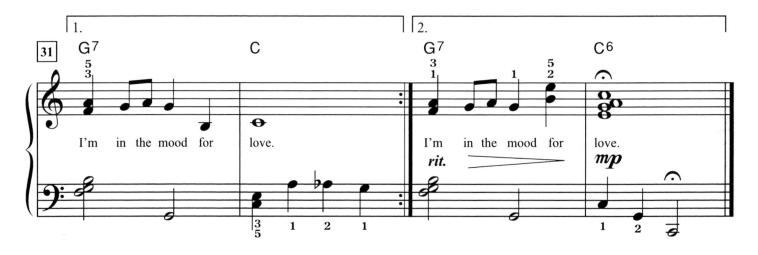

I'm in the mood for love. I'm in the mood for love.

THE LADY IS A TRAMP

Along with "My Funny Valentine" (page 168) and "Where or When" (page 228), "The Lady Is a Tramp" is from the 1937 musical *Babes in Arms.* Many singers from different decades have put their spin on this classic song that spoofs high society: Tommy Dorsey in the 1930s, Frank Sinatra in the 1940s, and Ella Fitzgerald in the 1950s, to name a few.

Words by Lorenz Hart
Music by Richard Rodgers
Arranged by Dan Coates

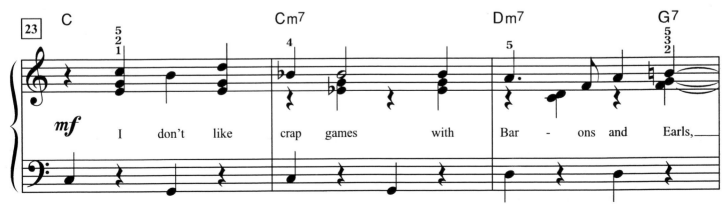

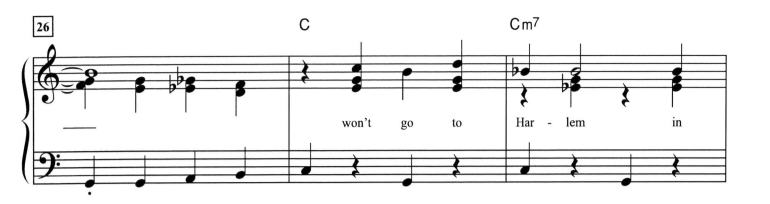

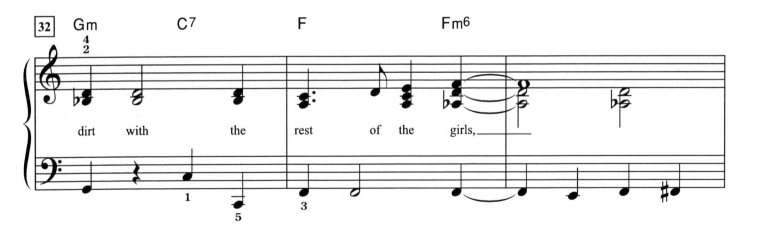

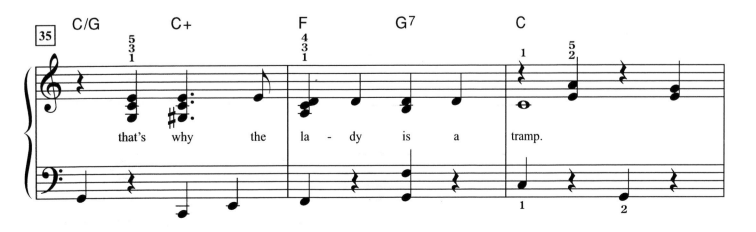

IT'S MY PARTY

Lesley Gore popularized "It's My Party" in 1963. Although it was Gore's only hit in the U.S., it reached #1 on both the pop and R & B charts. Gore also recorded a sequel to "It's My Party" entitled "Judy's Turn to Cry" in which the narrator of the first song gets revenge.

Words and Music by
Herb Wiener, John Gluck and Wally Gold
Arranged by Dan Coates

Moderately bright

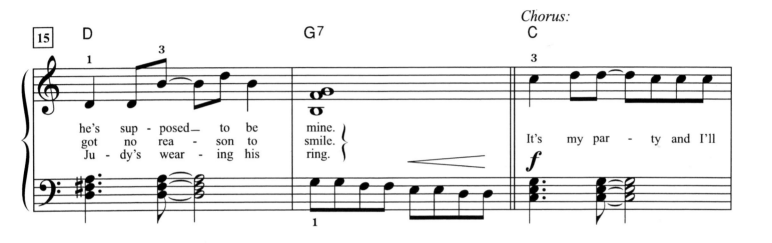

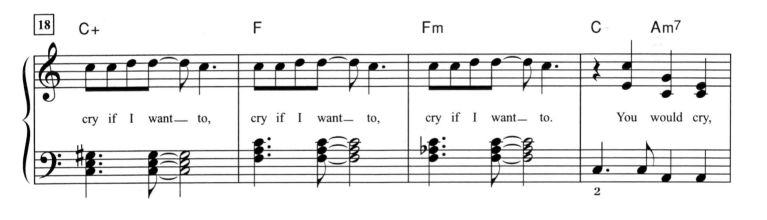

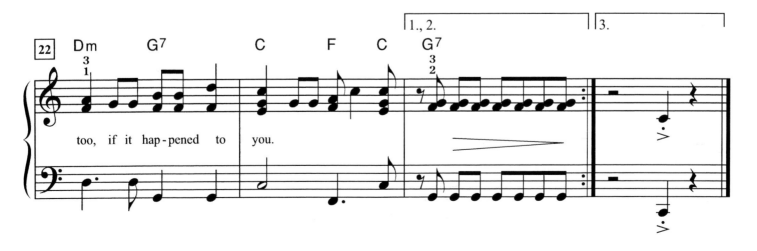

KILLING ME SOFTLY WITH HIS SONG

"Killing Me Softly with His Song" was written in 1971 and inspired by a poem by Lori Lieberman ("Killing Me Softly with His Blues") which she wrote after witnessing a live performance by Don McLean, the gifted folk rock singer who would later release the big hit "American Pie." Roberta Flack covered "Killing Me Softly with His Song" in 1973, a recording which won three Grammy Awards.

Words and Music by
Charles Fox and Norman Gimbel
Arranged by Dan Coates

LAURA

Laura (1944) is an Academy Award-winning film noir based on a popular 1943 detective novel by Vera Caspary. The film's brooding theme music was written by David Raksin, who composed it after he had unfortunately received a "Dear John" letter from his wife. Lyrics were added by Johnny Mercer, and the song has become a jazz standard having been recorded by hundreds of artists.

Lyrics by Johnny Mercer
Music by David Raksin
Arranged by Dan Coates

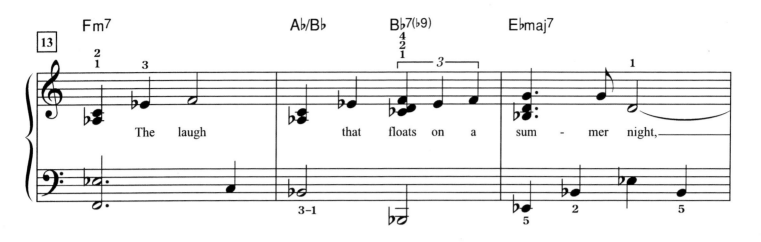

The laugh that floats on a sum - mer night,

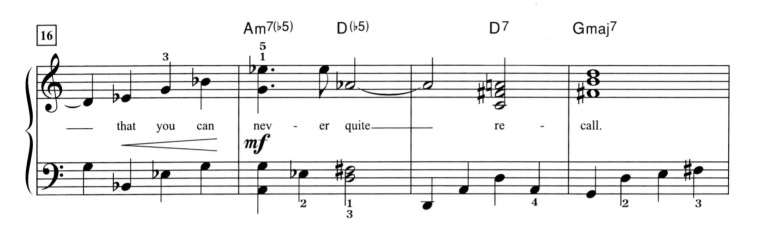

that you can nev - er quite re - call.

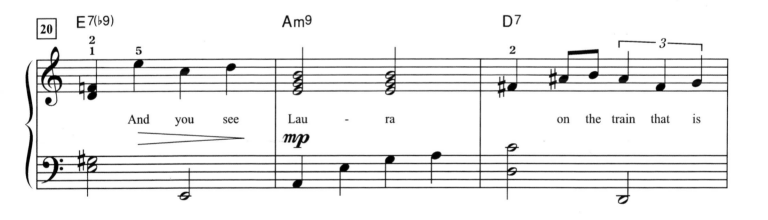

And you see Lau - ra on the train that is

pass - ing through. Those eyes,

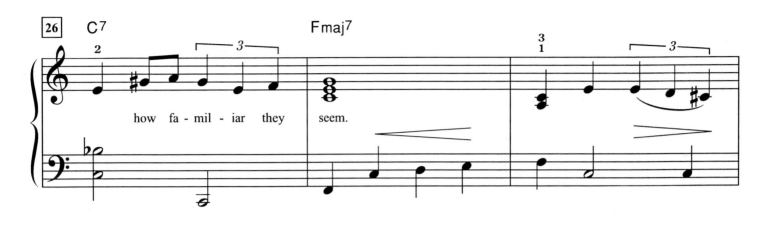

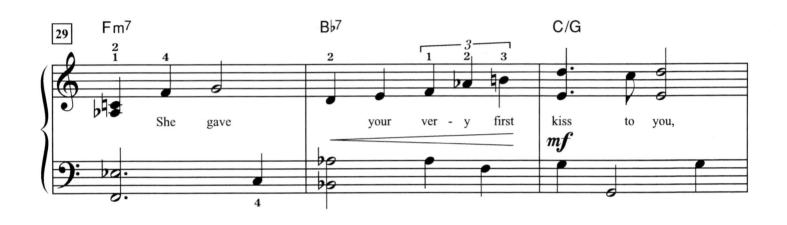

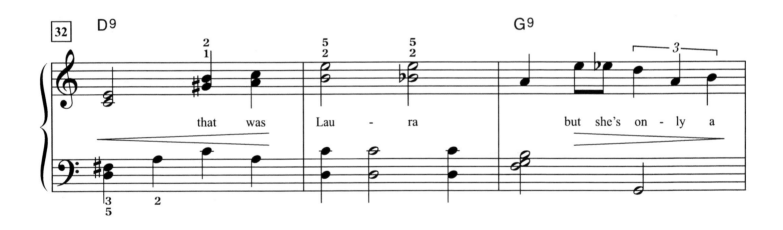

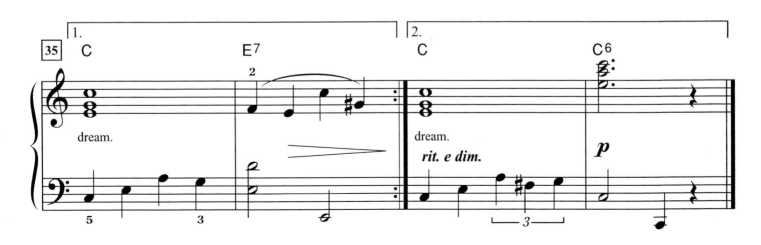

LEAVING ON A JET PLANE

Peter, Paul and Mary's huge 1969 hit single, "Leaving on a Jet Plane," was written by John Denver in an airport in Washington in 1967 while on a layover. Its original title was "Oh Babe I Hate to Go" but was changed by Denver at the suggestion of his producer, Milt Okun.

Words and Music by John Denver
Arranged by Dan Coates

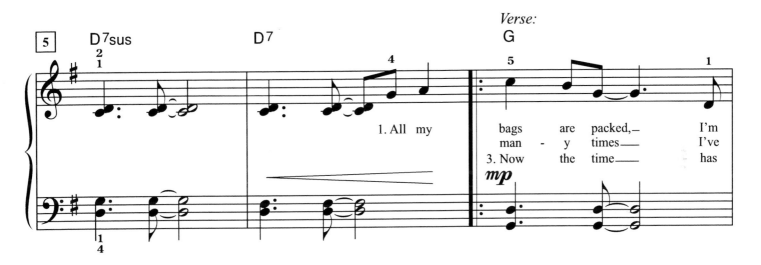

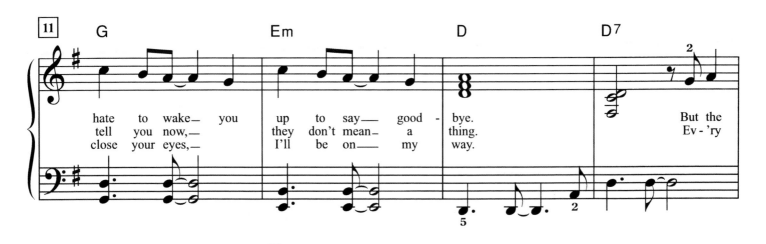

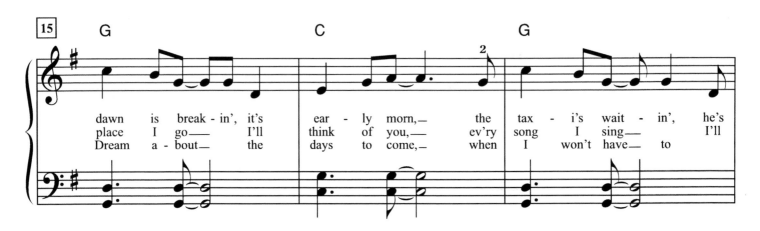

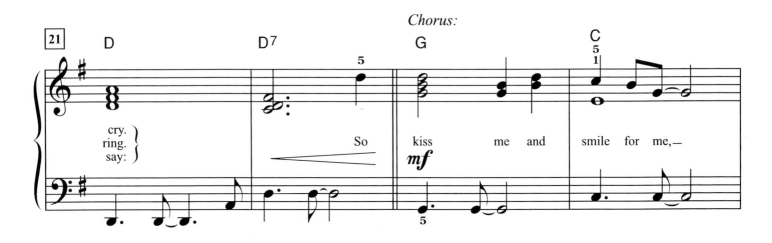

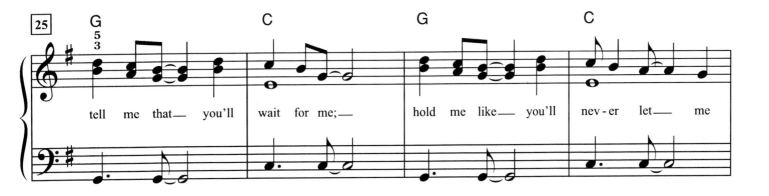

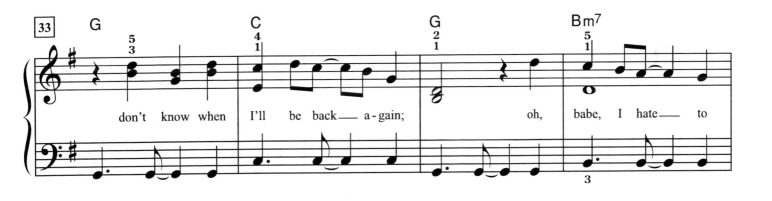

MISTY

"Misty" was originally composed as an instrumental jazz piece in 1954 by the legendary pianist Erroll Garner. Lyrics were later added and it went on to become one of the most recorded vocal jazz standards. Just a few of the artists who have recorded "Misty" are: Ella Fitzgerald, Frank Sinatra, Aretha Franklin, Freddie Hubbard, McCoy Tyner, Duke Ellington, Etta James, Julie London, Dave Koz, Jackie Gleason, Dexter Gordon, Johnny Mathis, Dianne Reeves, Kenny Rogers, Doc Severinsen, Sarah Vaughan, Oscar Peterson, Itzhak Perlman, Wes Montgomery, and many others.

Words by Johnny Burke
Music by Erroll Garner
Arranged by Dan Coates

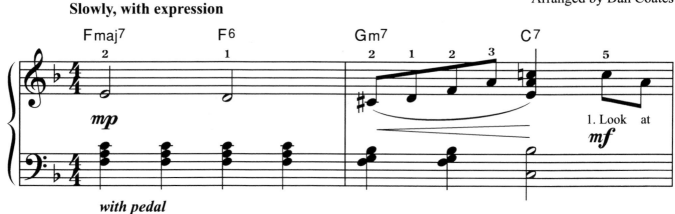

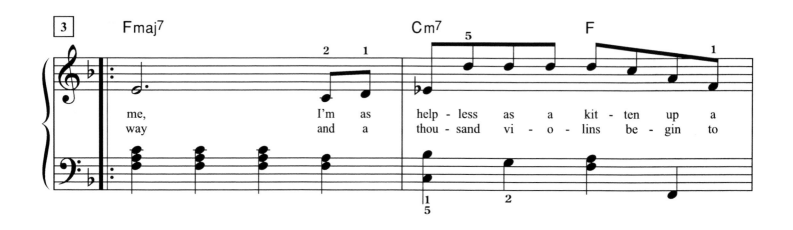

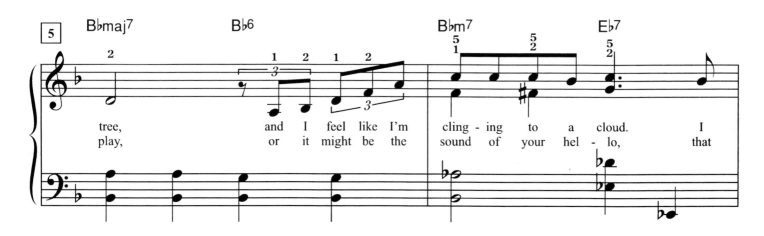

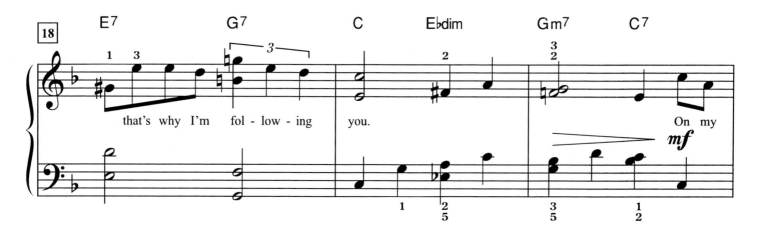

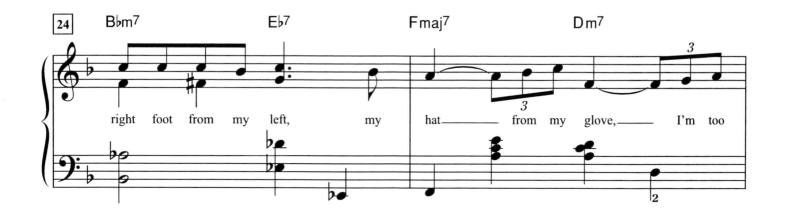

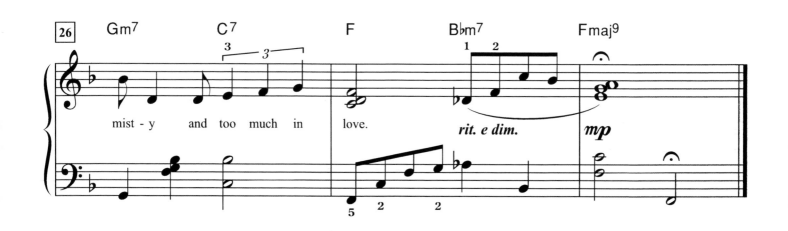

MOONLIGHT SERENADE

"Moonlight Serenade" was originally titled "Now I Lay Me Down to Weep" and released as the B-side to Glenn Miller's "Sunrise Serenade." The instrumental tune became a huge hit and Miller's signature song, capturing the big band sound of the 1940s. Lyrics were added by Mitchell Parish, and the song has been used in numerous films and on television.

Music by Glenn Miller
Lyric by Mitchell Parish
Arranged by Dan Coates

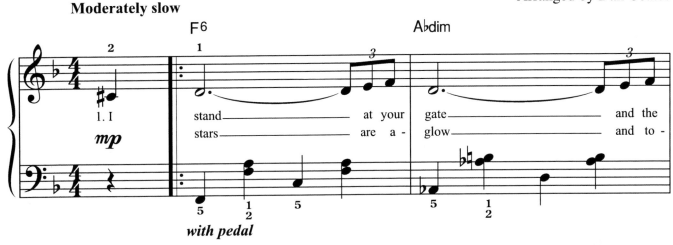

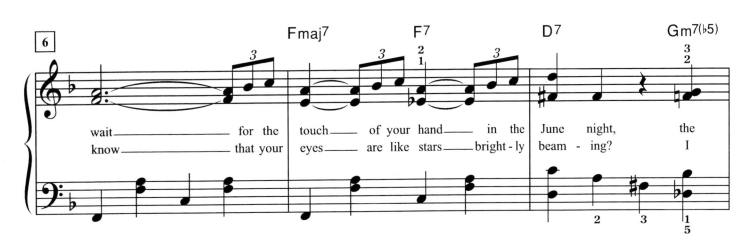

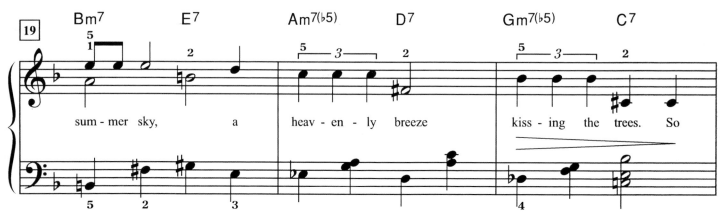

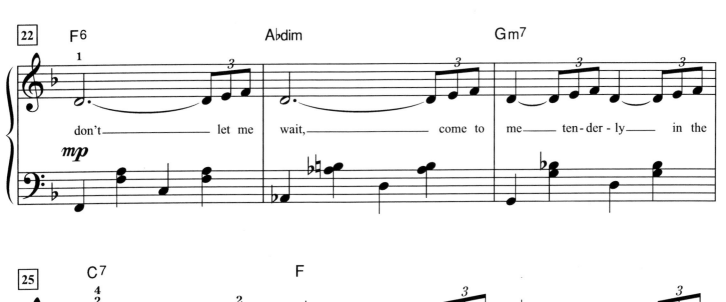

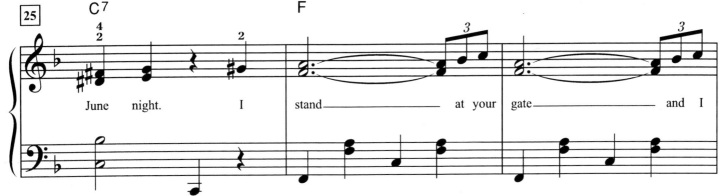

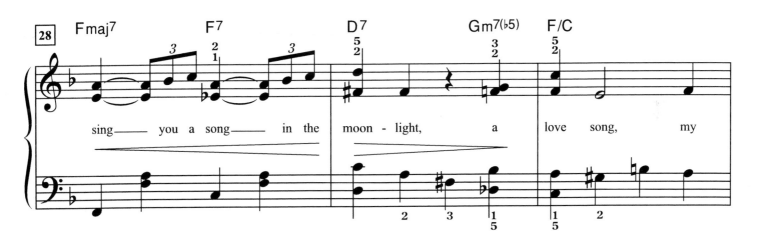

MOONDANCE

Rock and Roll Hall of Fame inductee Van Morrison released his third solo album *Moondance* in 1970, and the title song was released as a single in 1977. The album's songs center around life in the country and are a mix of R & B, country rock, and jazz.

Words and Music by Van Morrison
Arranged by Dan Coates

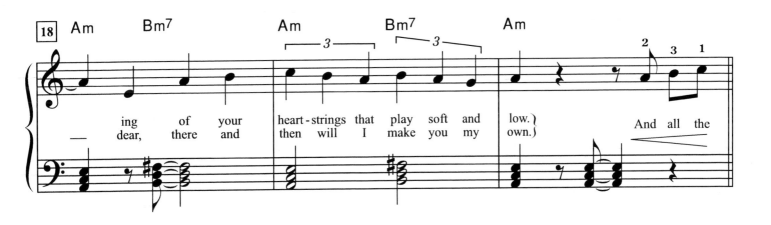

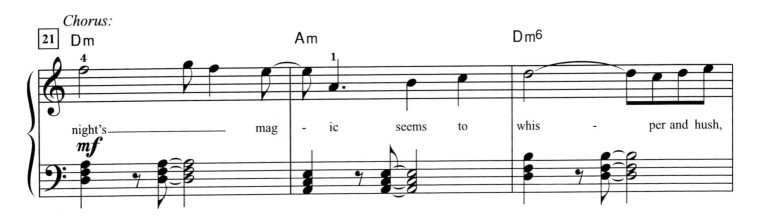

MY FUNNY VALENTINE

"My Funny Valentine"—another hit song from *Babes in Arms* (see "Where or When" on page 228)—has been recorded by countless artists: Barbra Streisand, Ella Fitzgerald, Frank Sinatra, Tony Bennett, Buddy Rich, Mel Tormé, Sammy Davis Jr., Stan Getz, Sarah Vaughan, Anita O'Day, and many others. Perhaps the most influential recording was a collaboration made in 1953 by the Gerry Mulligan Quartet and Chet Baker, a jazz trumpeter and velvet-voiced singer. This recording featured a memorable solo by Baker and soared to the top of the charts.

Words by Lorenz Hart
Music by Richard Rodgers
Arranged by Dan Coates

NIGHT AND DAY

"Night and Day" is one of Cole Porter's most popular compositions. It was originally written for his 1932 musical *Gay Divorce*, which starred Fred Astaire. More Americans were introduced to "Night and Day" through Astaire's performance of it in the film version of the musical, which was re-named *The Gay Divorcée*. In addition to Astaire, other singers including Frank Sinatra, Ella Fitzgerald, Ringo Starr, and U2 have all put their spin on this classic.

Words and Music by Cole Porter
Arranged by Dan Coates

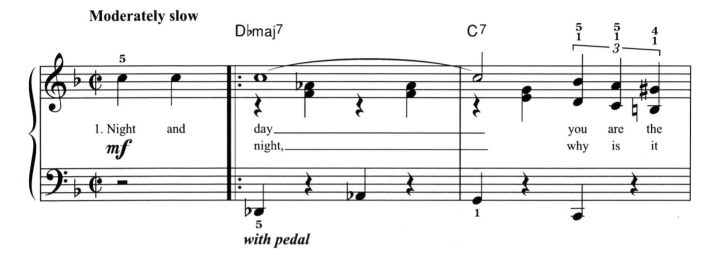

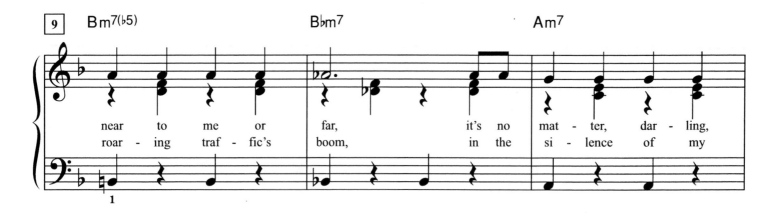

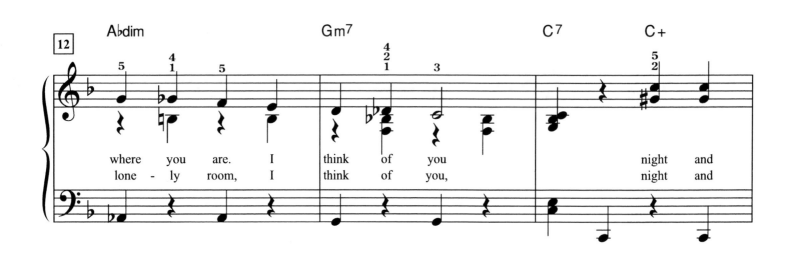

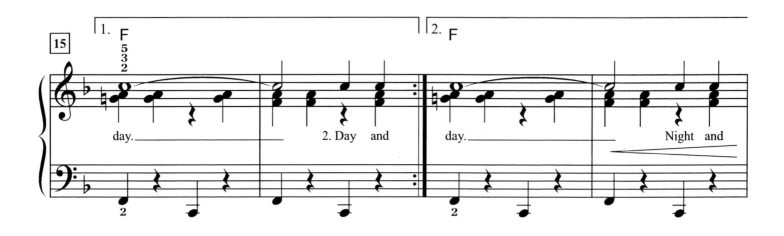

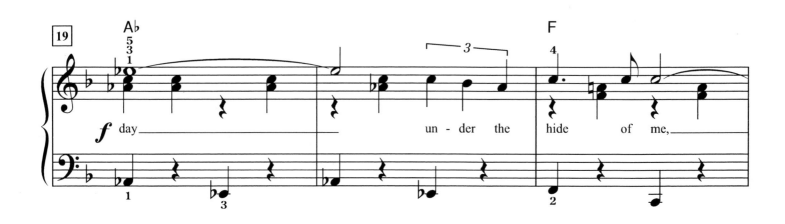

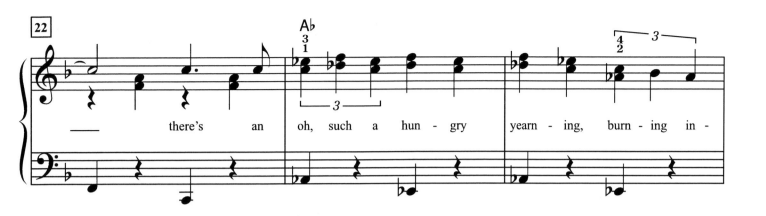

there's an oh, such a hun - gry yearn - ing, burn - ing in -

side of me. ____ And its tor - ment won't be

through 'til you let me spend my life mak - ing love to you,

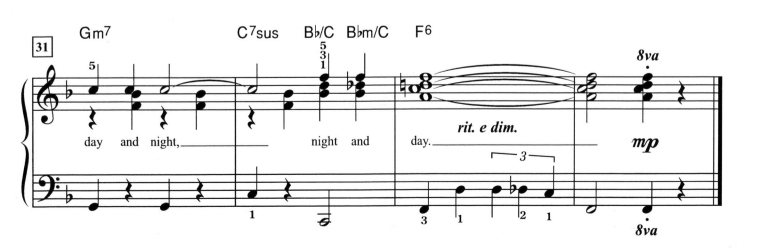

day and night, ____ night and day. ____

NEED YOU NOW

With its universally resonant theme of loneliness and longing, "Need You Now" catapulted pop-country trio Lady Antebellum to international super-stardom. The band's label executives, concerned about potential controversy, were reportedly uneasy at first about the song's lyrical references to being "a little drunk," but decided to allow the words to remain unaltered. Considering the song went on to win four Grammy® awards in 2011, including Song of the Year and Record of the Year, it's unlikely that they had any regrets.

Words and Music by
Dave Haywood, Charles Kelley,
Hillary Scott and Josh Kear
Arranged by Dan Coates

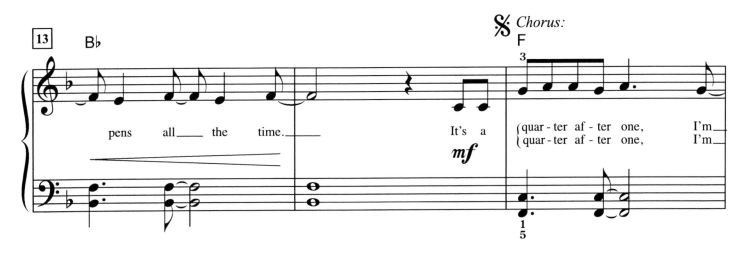

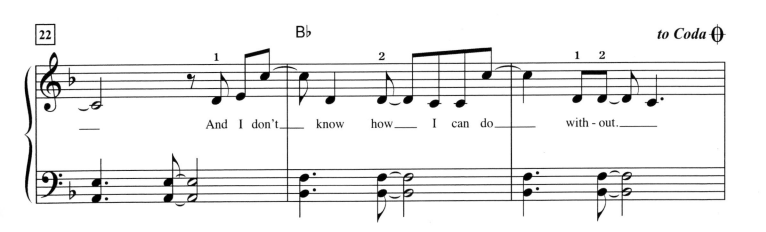

Verse 2:
Another shot of whiskey, can't stop looking at the door,
Wishing you'd come sweeping in the way you did before.
And I wonder if I ever cross your mind.
For me it happens all the time.
(To Chorus:)

OVER THE RAINBOW

"Over the Rainbow" was featured in MGM's classic 1939 film *The Wizard of Oz*. It was famously sung in the film by Judy Garland who played Dorothy, a Kansas farm girl who yearns for a better life. "Over the Rainbow" has been voted the #1 movie song by the American Film Institute. In addition to being the signature song for Garland, it has also been the signature song for two great singers whose lives and careers ended prematurely—Eva Cassidy and Israel "Iz" Kamakawiwo'ole.

Music by Harold Arlen
Lyrics by E.Y. Harburg
Arranged by Dan Coates

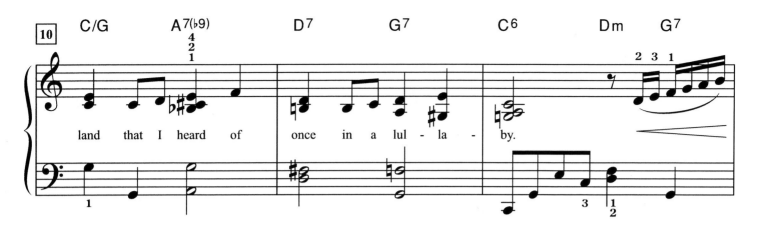

land that I heard of once in a lul - la - by.

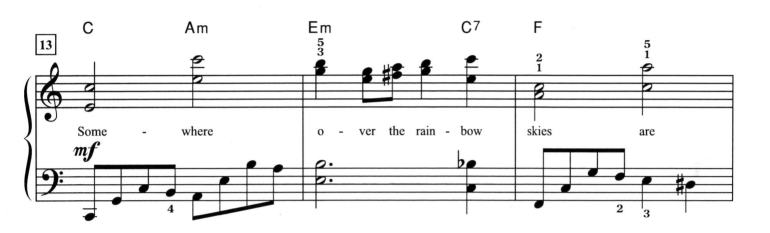

Some - where o - ver the rain - bow skies are

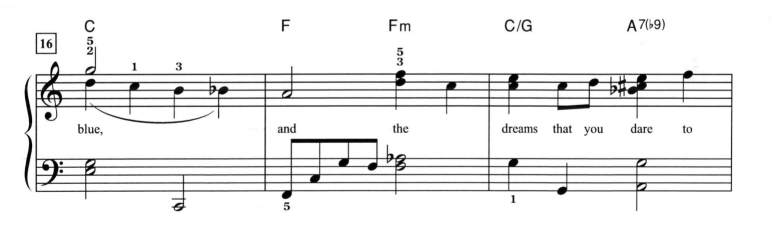

blue, and the dreams that you dare to

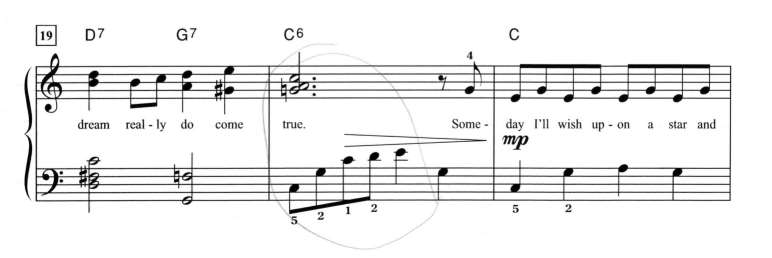

dream real - ly do come true. Some - day I'll wish up - on a star and

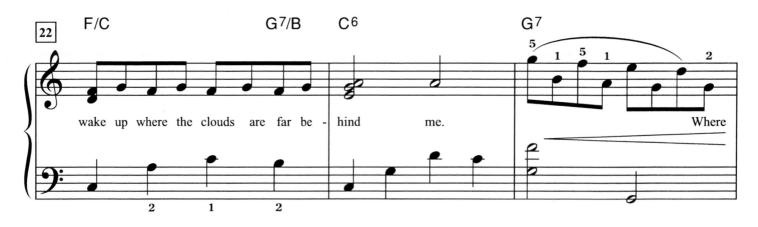

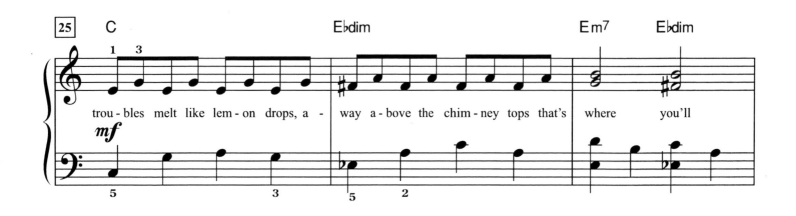

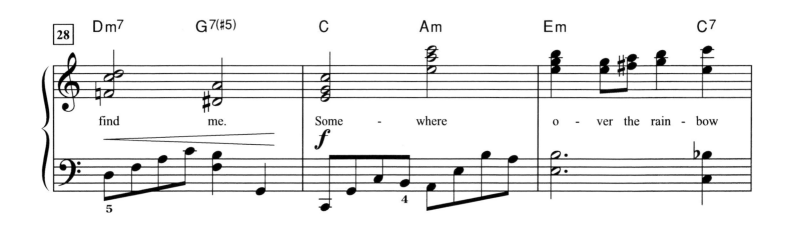

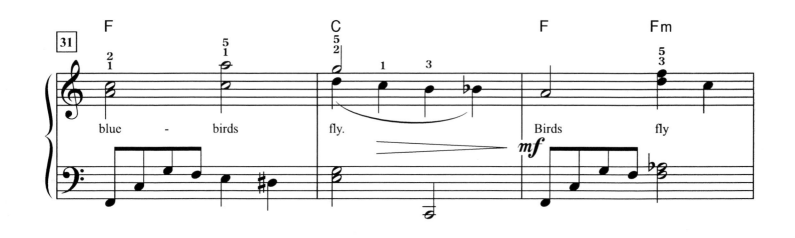

o - ver the rain - bow, why then, oh why can't I?

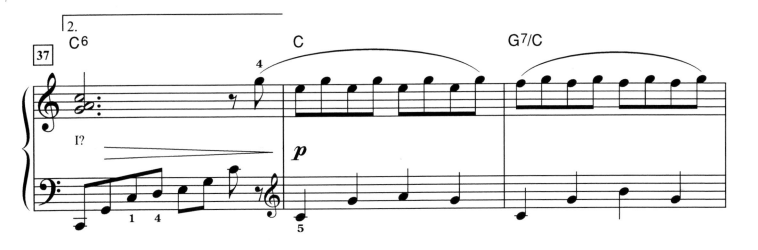

I?

If hap - py lit - tle blue - birds fly be -

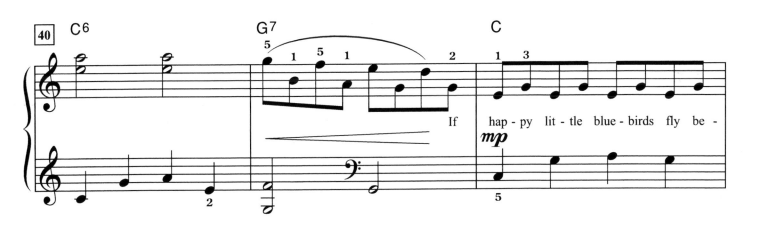

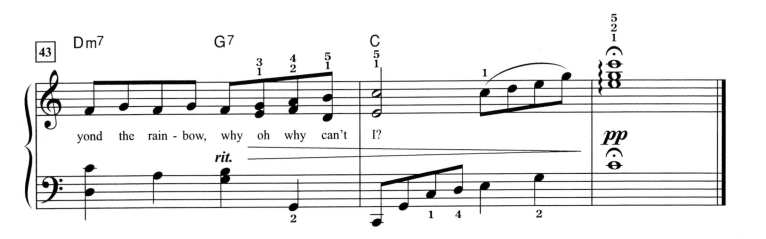

yond the rain - bow, why oh why can't I?

THE PINK PANTHER

The Pink Panther is a series of comedic films spanning the years 1963–2006. The main character is bumbling French detective, Jacques Clouseau (famously played by Peter Sellars in the earlier films), who manages to survive countless brushes with death despite his clumsiness and aloof demeanor. The jazzy theme is famous for its chromatically moving parallel fifths and furtive character.

Music by Henry Mancini
Arranged by Dan Coates

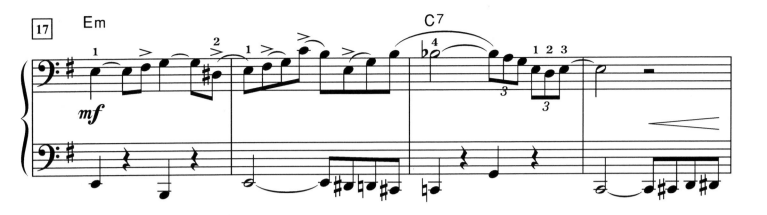

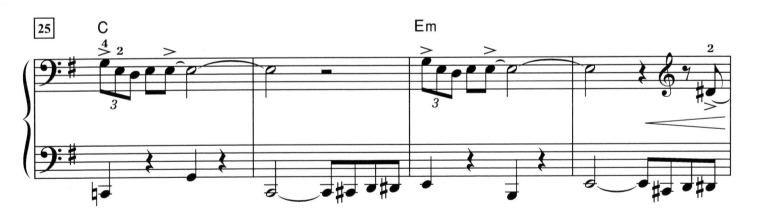

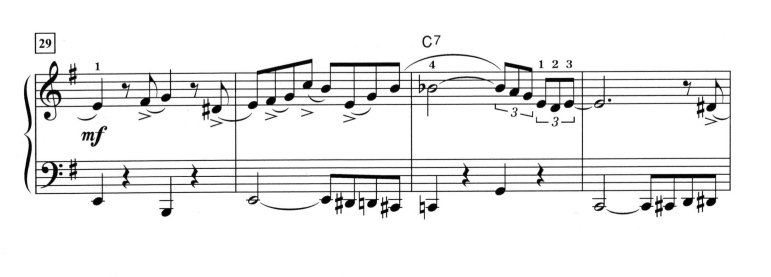

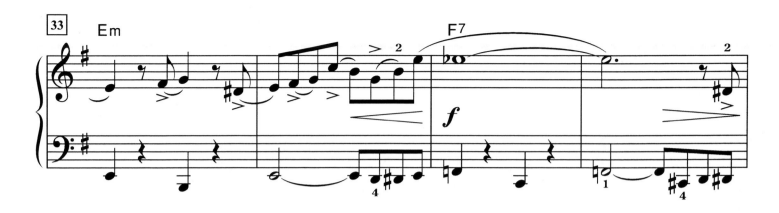

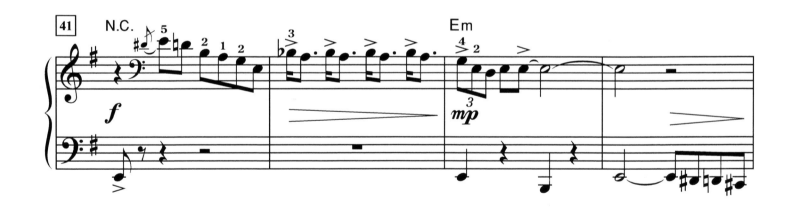

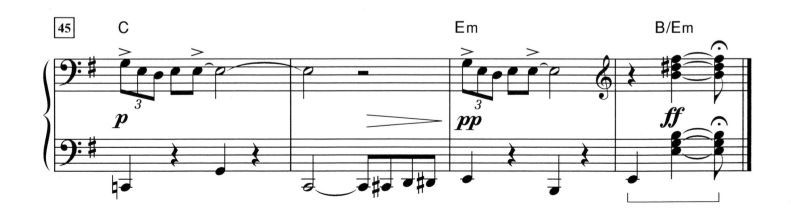

THE PRAYER

"The Prayer" was recorded by Canadian superstar Céline Dion and Italian tenor Andrea Bocelli in 1998, both as a duet and as solo performances. It was on the *Quest for Camelot* soundtrack, won a Golden Globe award for Best Original Song, and was also nominated for an Academy Award. The song was also covered in 2004 by *Australian Idol* runner up Anthony Callea and quickly became the fastest-selling single to be released by an Australian artist.

Words and Music by
Carole Bayer Sager and David Foster
Italian Lyric by Alberto Testa and Tony Renis
Arranged by Dan Coates

Slowly, with expression

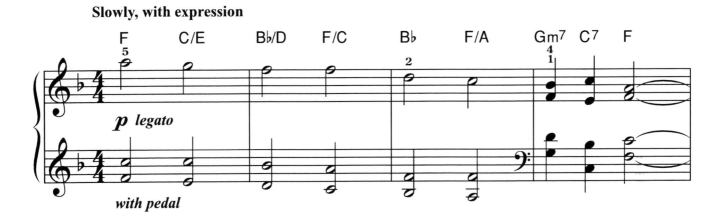

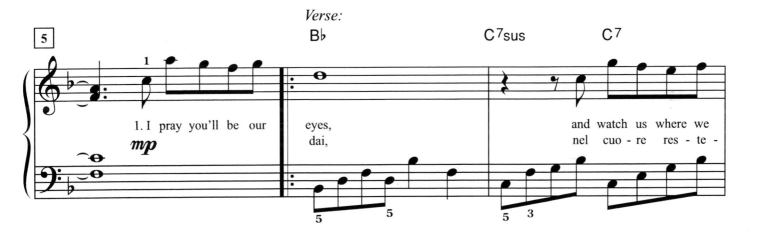

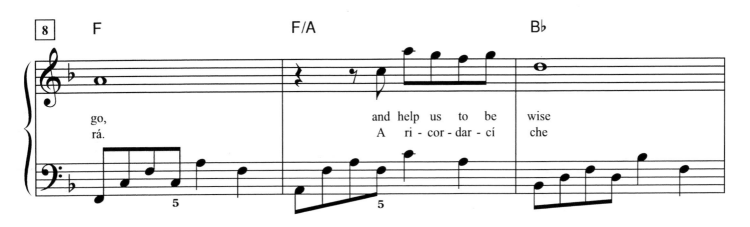

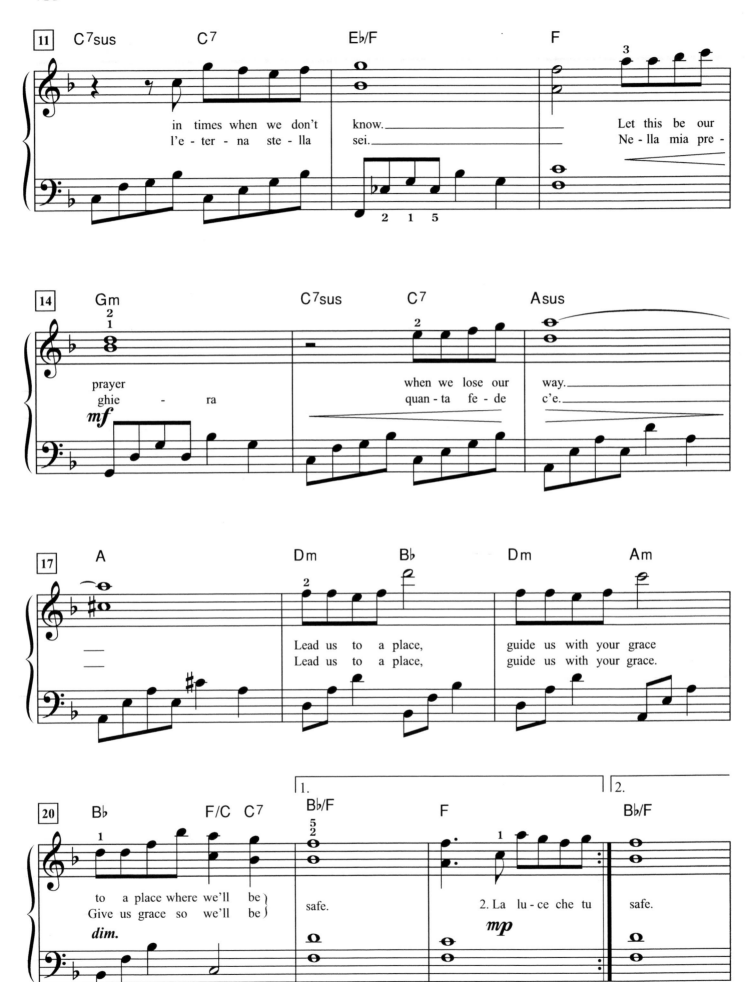

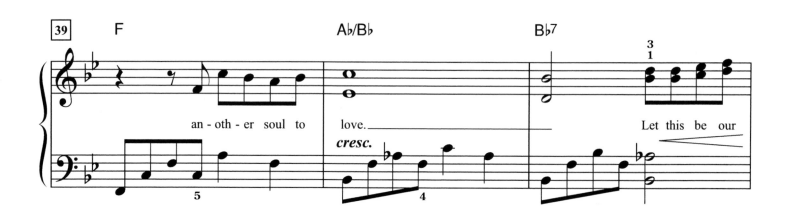

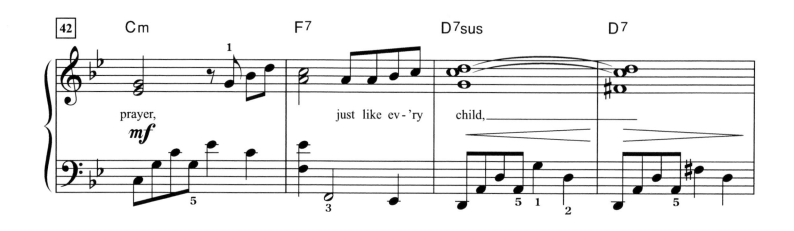

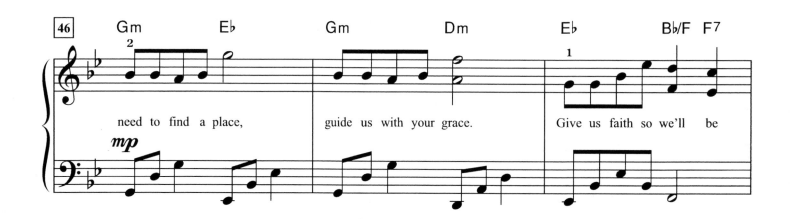

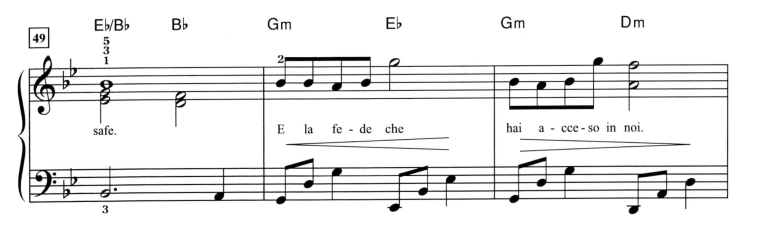

Verse 2 (English lyric):
I pray we'll find your light,
And hold it in our hearts
When stars go out each night.
Let this be our prayer,
When shadows fill our day.
Lead us to a place,
Guide us with your grace.
Give us faith so we'll be safe.

Verse 3 (Italian lyric):
La forza che ci dai
é il desiderio che.
Ognuno trovi amore
Intorno e dentro sé.

(WE'RE GONNA) ROCK AROUND THE CLOCK

"(We're Gonna) Rock Around the Clock" is considered the first rock and roll song. The most famous version was recorded by Bill Haley & His Comets in 1954. However, it did not hit the pop charts until it played during the opening credits of the 1955 film *Blackboard Jungle*. Following its film "debut," it topped the American Billboard charts for eight weeks.

Words and Music by
Max C. Freedman and Jimmy De Knight
Arranged by Dan Coates

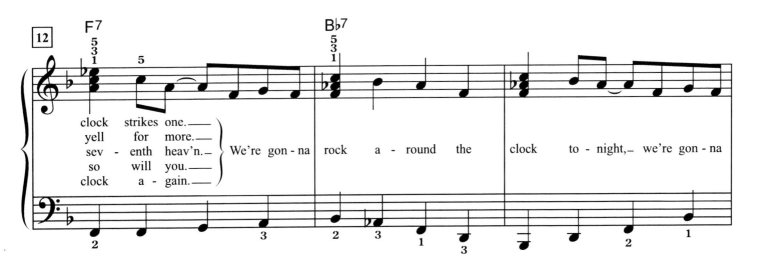

clock strikes one.—
yell for more.—
sev - enth heav'n.— } We're gon-na rock a - round the clock to-night,— we're gon - na
so will you.—
clock a - gain.—

rock, rock, rock 'til broad day - light.— We're gon-na rock, gon - na rock a -

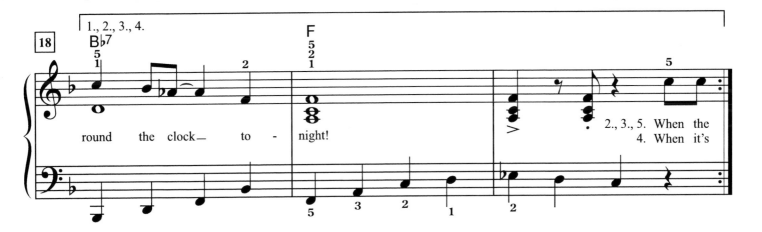

1., 2., 3., 4.

round the clock— to - night! 2., 3., 5. When the
4. When it's

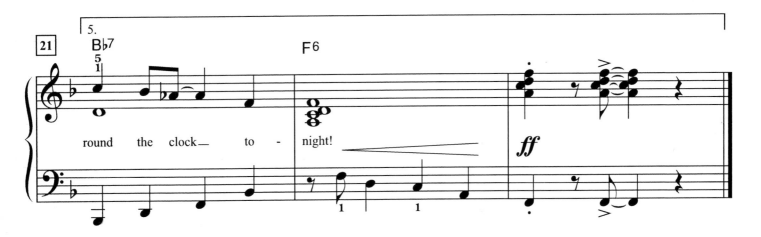

5.

round the clock— to - night!— ff

THE SHADOW OF YOUR SMILE

In 1965 Vincente Minnelli directed Richard Burton and Elizabeth Taylor in *The Sandpiper*, a story about a single mother who has a romance with the headmaster of a boarding school. Their love theme, "The Shadow of Your Smile," won the Academy Award for Best Original Song. Since then, it has been performed and recorded by many singing legends: Tony Bennett, Barbra Streisand, Perry Como, and Frank Sinatra, to name a few.

Music by Johnny Mandel
Lyric by Paul Francis Webster
Arranged by Dan Coates

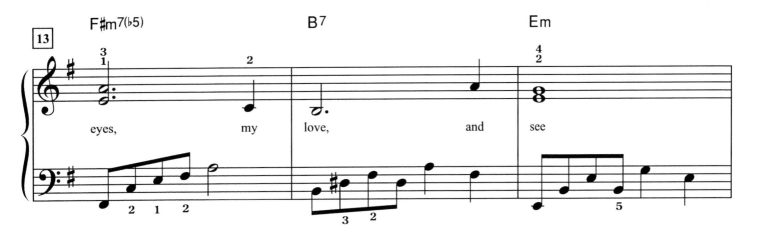

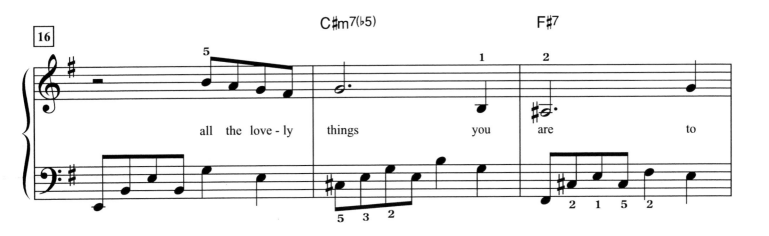

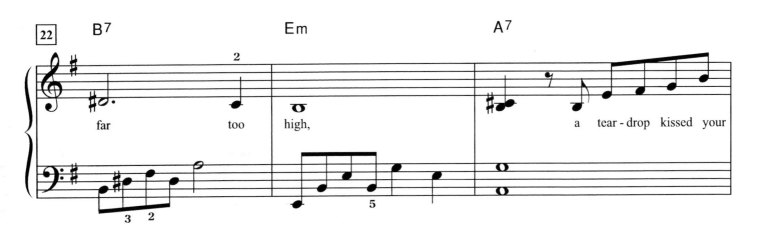

SINGIN' IN THE RAIN
(FROM "SINGIN' IN THE RAIN")

Before Arthur Freed became one of the most successful producers of all time—bringing the world classic MGM musical movies such as *Babes in Arms, Meet Me in St. Louis, Annie Get Your Gun, Show Boat,* and *Brigadoon,* to name just a few—he worked as a pianist, a vaudeville performer, and a songwriter. Nacio Herb Brown followed a much different path, working as a tailor and realtor before becoming a full-time composer. MGM hired the two songwriters around the time that movies began to include sound. Their most popular hit is "Singin' in the Rain," which was famously performed by Gene Kelly in MGM's *Singin' in the Rain* (1952).

Music by Nacio Herb Brown
Lyric by Arthur Freed
Arranged by Dan Coates

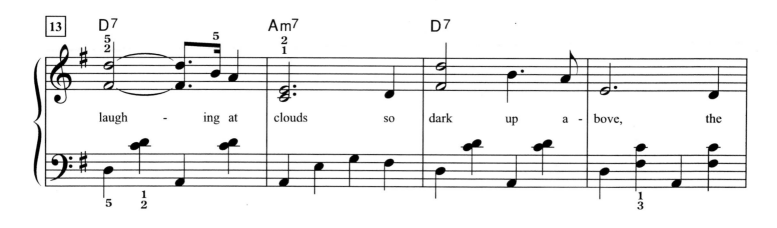

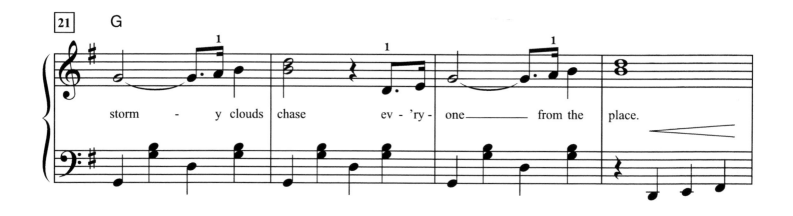

walk down the lane with a hap - py re - frain, and

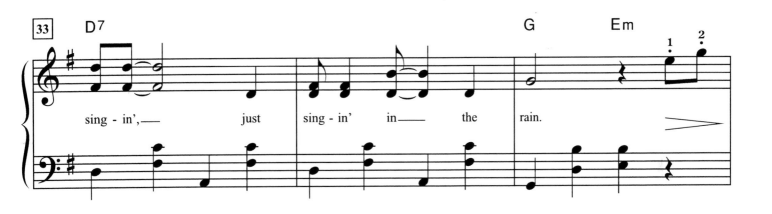

sing - in', __ just sing - in' in __ the rain.

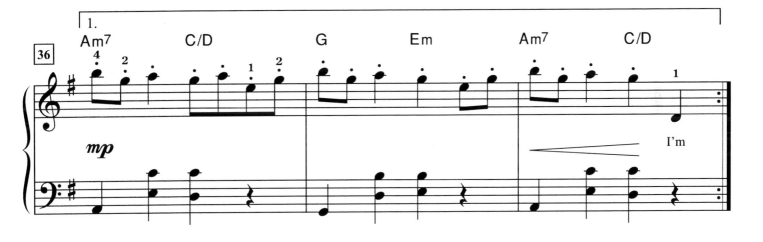

I'm

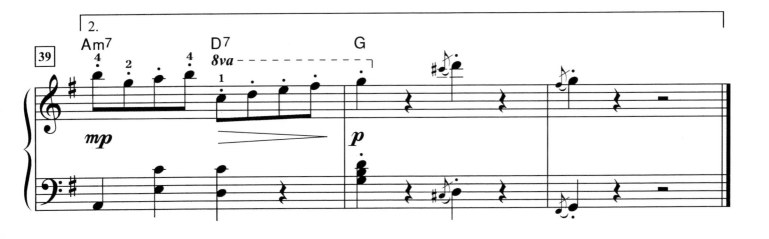

SH-BOOM
(LIFE COULD BE A DREAM)

"Sh-Boom" is considered by many to be the first, well-known doo-wop song. Doo-wop was a style of vocal music made popular in the 1950s. It takes its name from the nonsense syllables that are sung (like "sh-boom"). The original version hit #3 on the R & B charts and #9 on the pop charts. The most famous version is by The Crew Cuts who performed "Sh-Boom" on the Ed Sullivan show. Their version hit #1 on the Billboard charts in 1954.

Words and Music by
James Keyes, Carl Feaster, Floyd McRae,
Claude Feaster and James Edwards
Arranged by Dan Coates

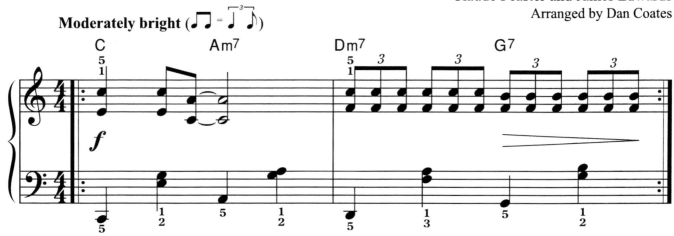

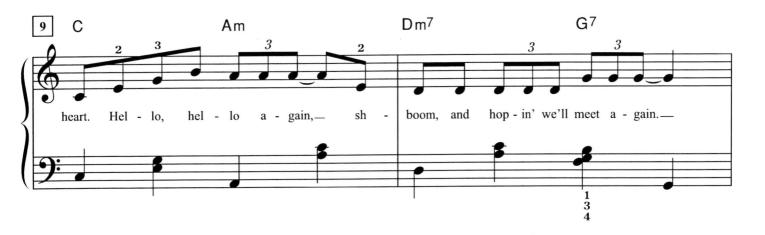

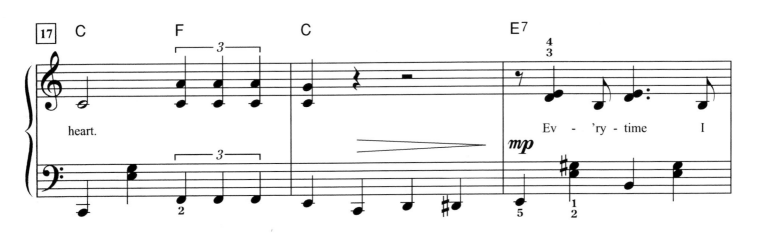

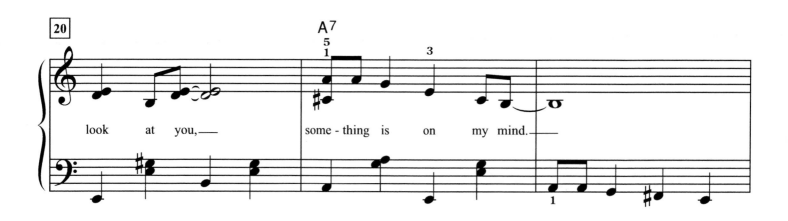

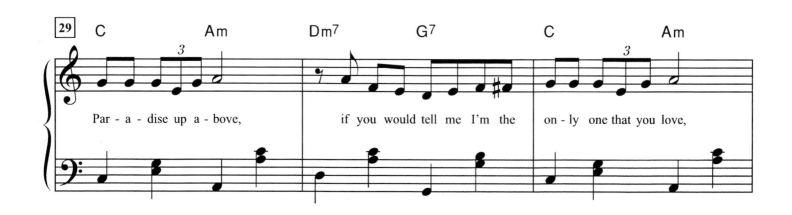

SONG FROM M*A*S*H
(Suicide Is Painless)

M*A*S*H is a 1970 comedic film by director Robert Altman about medical personnel at a Mobile Army Surgical Hospital (MASH). The film was based on a novel by Richard Hooker, *MASH: A Novel About Three Army Doctors*, set against the backdrop of the Korean War. The film was turned into a television series of the same name which ran on CBS from 1972 to 1983 and garnered a total of 14 Emmy Awards. The series finale was the most-watched television broadcast in history. The theme music was written by Johnny Mandel with lyrics written by Altman's 14-year-old son, Mike Altman.

Words and Music by
Mike Altman and Johnny Mandel
Arranged by Dan Coates

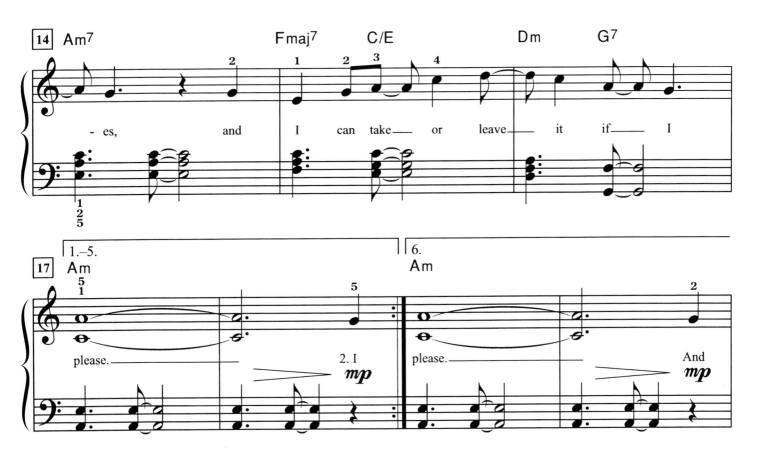

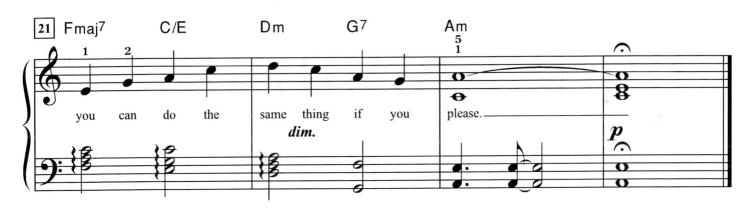

Verse 2:
I try to find a way to make
All our little joys relate
Without that ever-present hate
But now I know that it's too late.
And *(To Chorus:)*

Verse 3:
The game of life is hard to play,
I'm going to lose it anyway,
The losing card I'll someday lay,
So that is all I have to say,
That *(To Chorus:)*

Verse 4:
The only way you win is cheat,
And lay it down before I'm beat,
And to another give a seat,
For that's the only painless feat.
'Cause *(To Chorus:)*

Verse 5:
The sword of time will pierce our skins,
It doesn't hurt when it begins,
But as it works its way on in
The pain grows stronger, watch it grin.
For *(To Chorus:)*

Verse 6:
A brave man once requested me
To answer questions that are key,
Is it to be or not to be?
And I replied, "Oh, why ask me?"
'Cause *(To Chorus:)*

STAR WARS (MAIN TITLE)

On May 25, 1977 George Lucas introduced the world to *Star Wars,* one of the most successful, popular and influential films of all time, a science fiction masterpiece. The movie's dazzling special effects not only won over an ongoing fan base but also directed the film industry's focus to big-budget blockbuster productions. The film's soundtrack—performed by the London Symphony Orchestra with John Williams conducting—was voted #1 by the American Film Institute in 2005.

By **JOHN WILLIAMS**
Arranged by Dan Coates

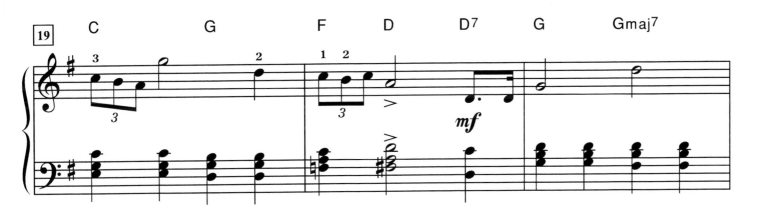

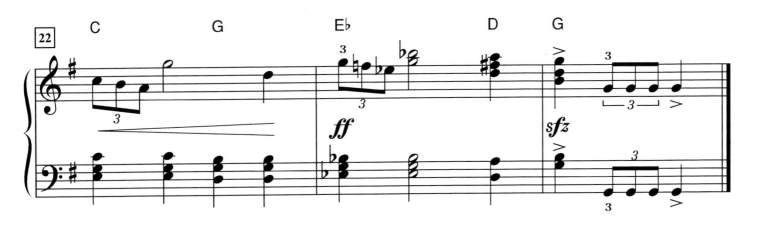

A STRING OF PEARLS

The F. W. Woolworth company was a retail company that was one of the original American five-and-dime stores. Founded in 1878 by Frank Winfield Woolworth, Woolworth's (as it became known) was one of the first stores to display products for customers to handle without the assistance of a sales clerk. In 1941 while working in Glenn Miller's band, Jerry Gray composed "String of Pearls" which became his most successful song. Lyrics were added by Eddie DeLange that describe a love sparked at Woolworth's.

Music by Jerry Gray
Words by Eddie DeLange
Arranged by Dan Coates

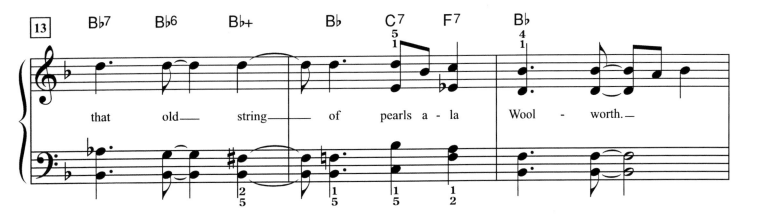

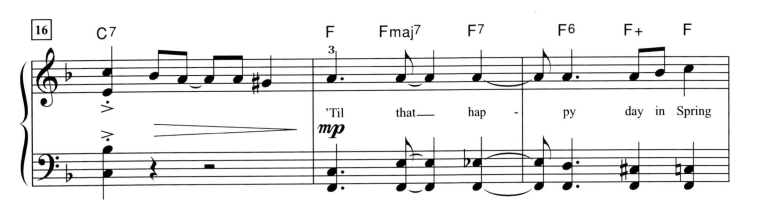

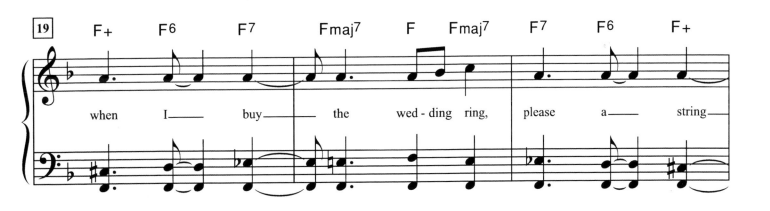

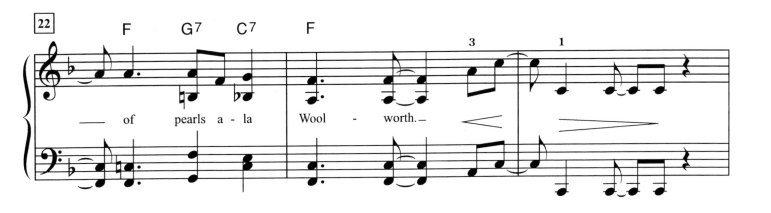

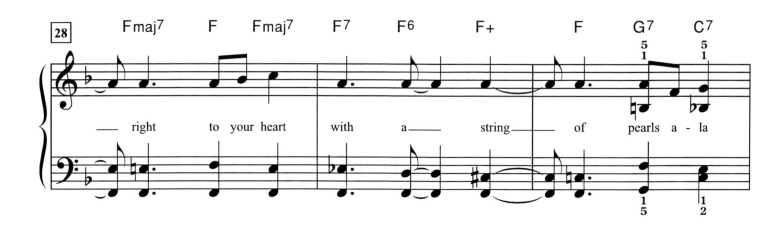

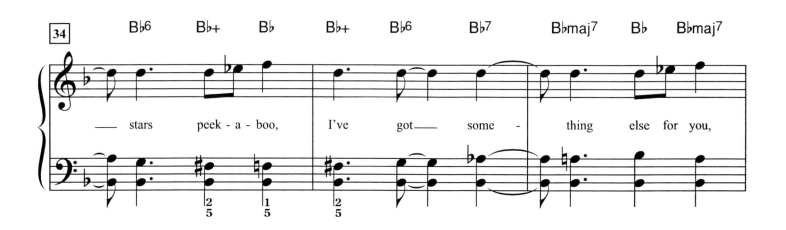

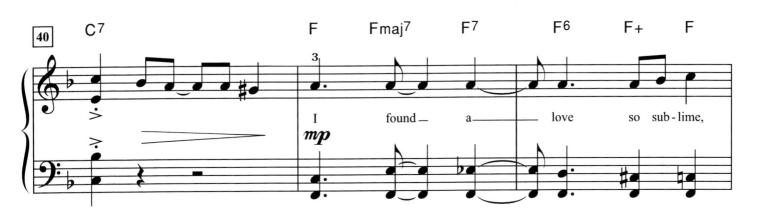

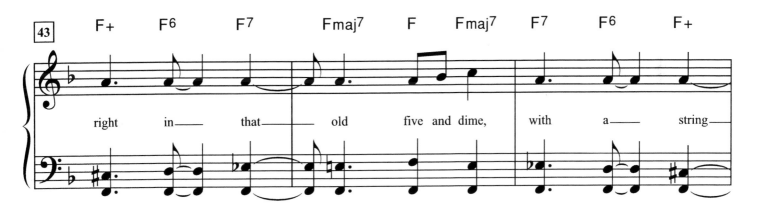

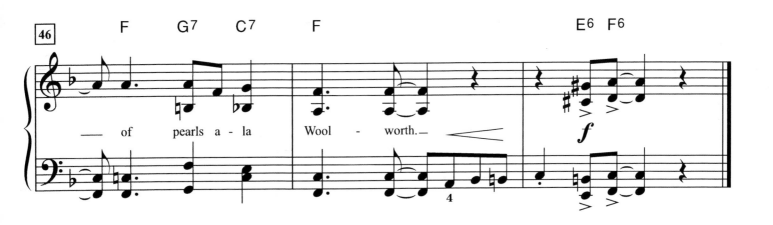

SUMMERTIME

"Summertime" was originally written as an aria for the opera *Porgy and Bess*. In the opera, it is one of the first arias and is sung as a lullaby. The song has since become a staple, not only in the world of opera but also in pop and jazz. Many renditions have made their way into the mainstream by artists such as Janis Joplin, Billie Holiday, and Nina Simone. There is also a famous collaborative recording by Ella Fitzgerald and Louis Armstrong.

Music and Lyrics by George Gershwin,
DuBose and Dorothy Heyward and Ira Gershwin
Arranged by Dan Coates

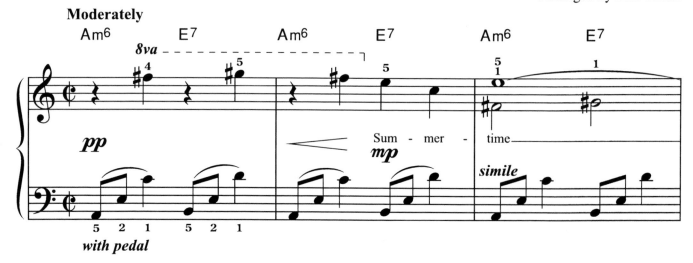

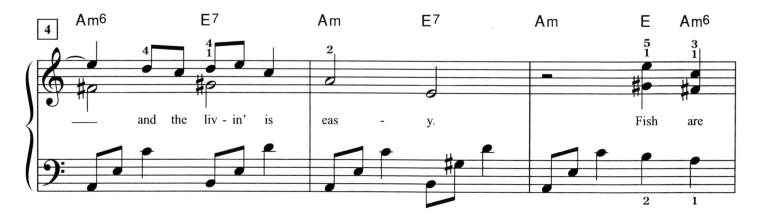

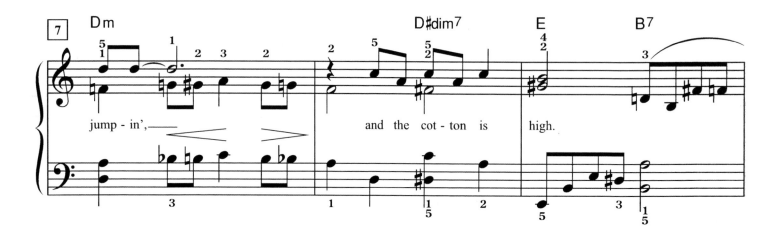

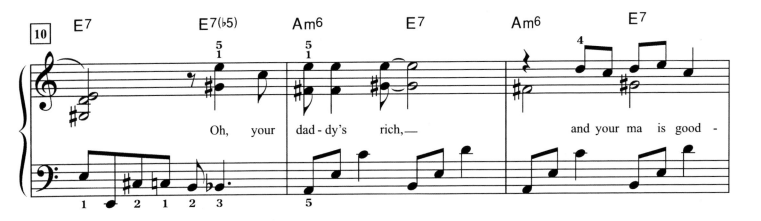

Oh, your dad-dy's rich,— and your ma is good -

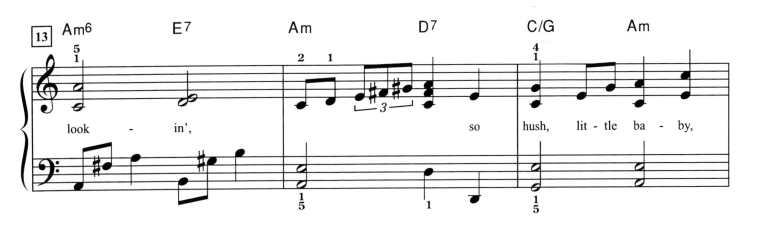

look - in', so hush, lit - tle ba - by,

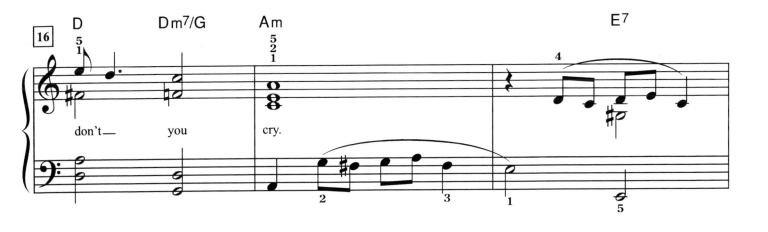

don't— you cry.

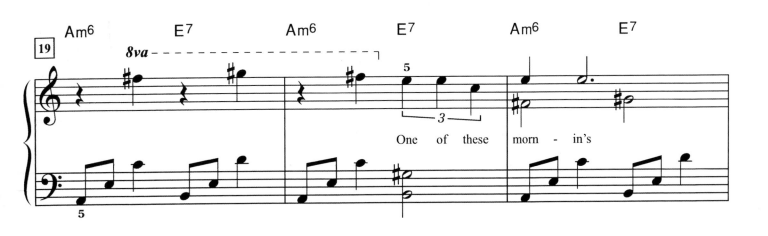

One of these morn - in's

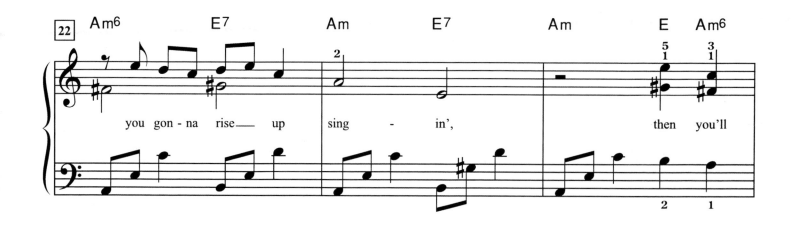

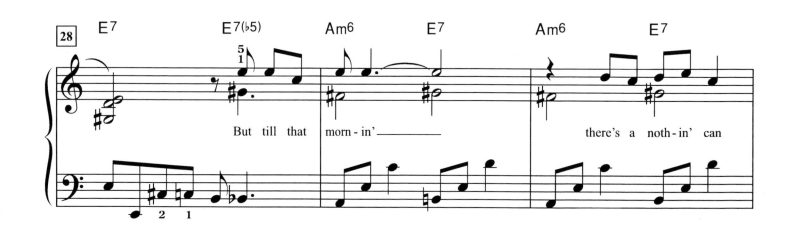

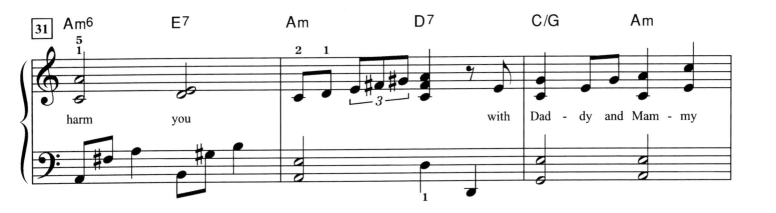

harm you

with Dad - dy and Mam - my

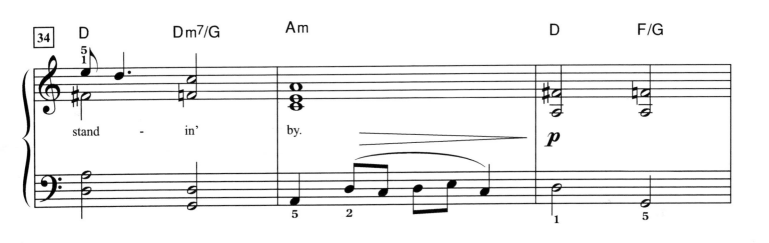

stand - in'

by.

p

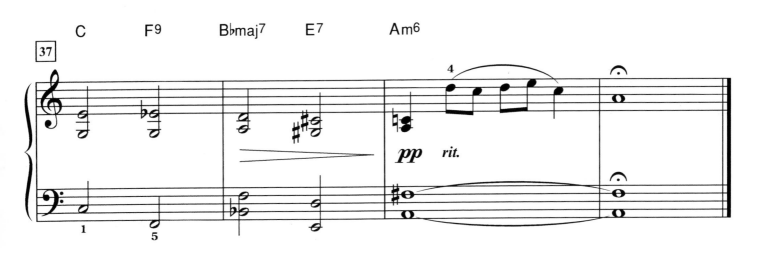

pp *rit.*

SOMEONE TO WATCH OVER ME
(FROM *OH, KAY*)

Prohibition in the United States (1920–1933) greatly influenced the arts both before and after its repeal. *Oh, Kay* opened on Broadway in 1926, at the height of Prohibition, and comically portrayed a love story between Kay, an English bootlegger (alcohol smuggler), and Jimmy, a wealthy New Yorker. The bootlegger was played by Gertrude Lawrence, one of the first English actresses to perform on Broadway. She sang "Someone to Watch Over Me" in the second act while her character holds a rag doll and dreams of a better life with Jimmy. Since then, the song has become a standard and has been recorded by many legendary singers.

Music and Lyrics by George Gershwin and Ira Gershwin
Arranged by Dan Coates

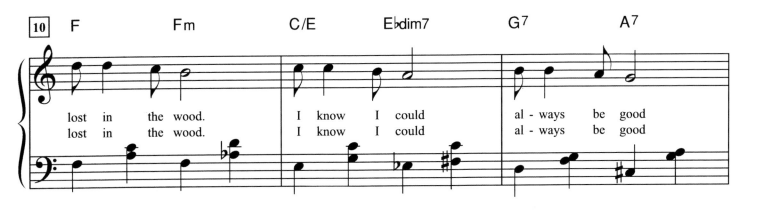

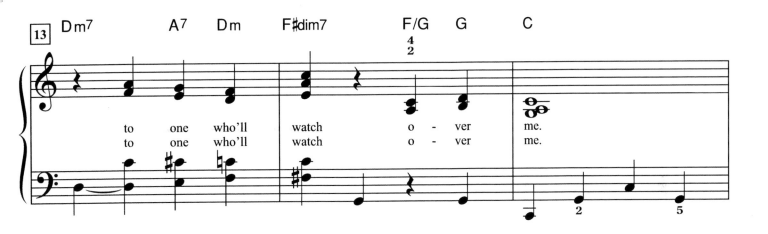

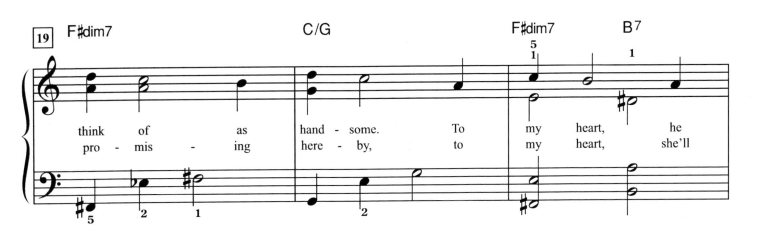

THE TROLLEY SONG

"The Trolley Song" was made famous by Judy Garland in the 1944 film *Meet Me in St. Louis*. The movie was adapted from a series of short stories published in *The New Yorker* magazine by Sally Benson. The plot tells the story of four sisters living in St. Louis around the time of the 1904 World's Fair. Towards the end of the movie, Garland's character sings another famous song to console one of her sisters—"Have Yourself a Merry Little Christmas."

Music by Ralph Blane
Lyrics by Hugh Martin
Arranged by Dan Coates

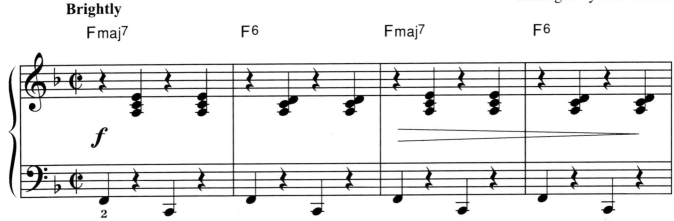

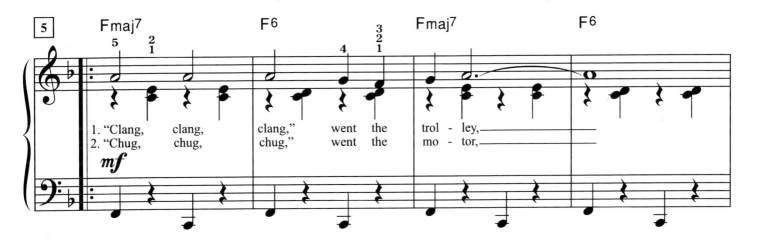

1. "Clang, clang, clang," went the trol-ley,
2. "Chug, chug, chug," went the mo-tor,

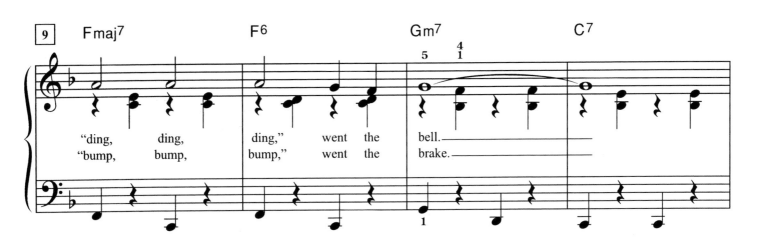

"ding, ding, ding," went the bell.
"bump, bump, bump," went the brake.

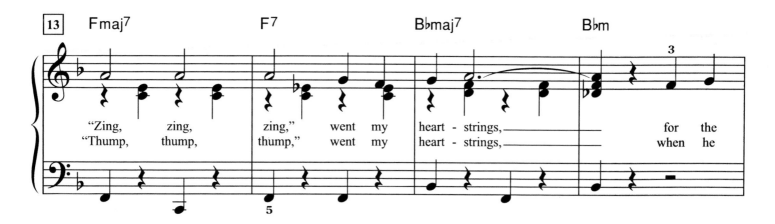

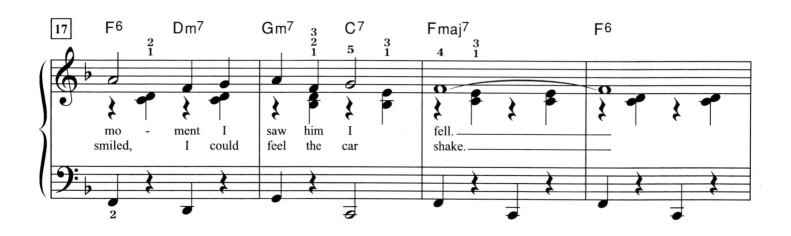

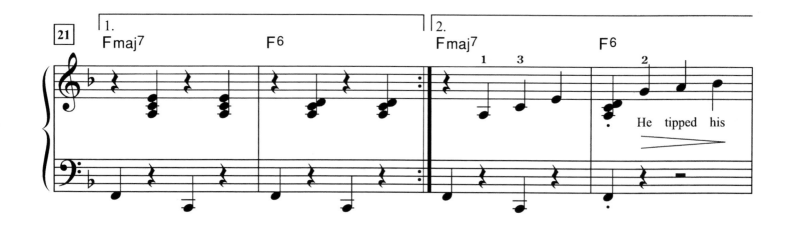

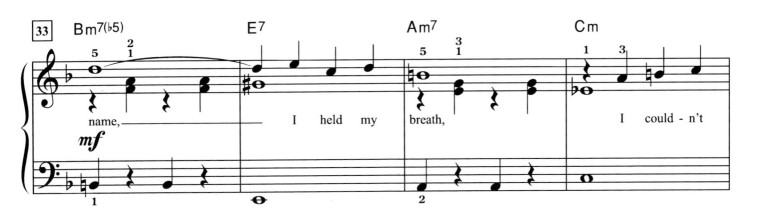

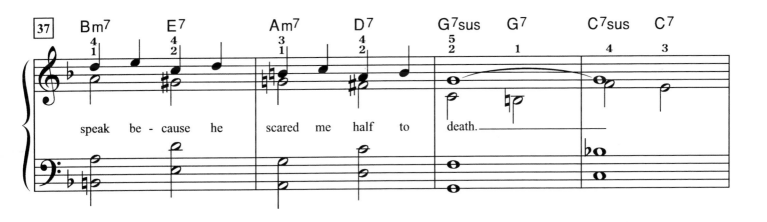

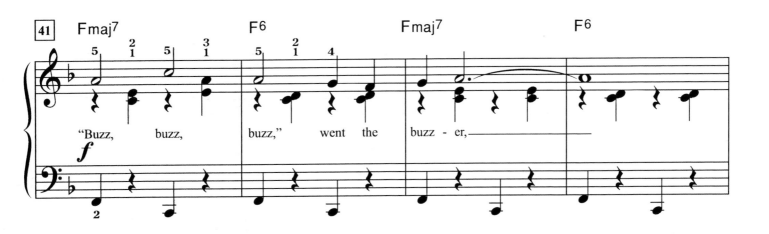

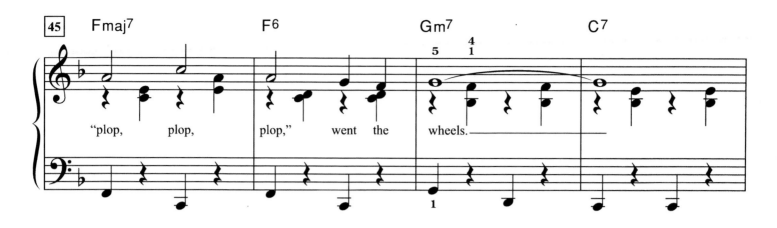

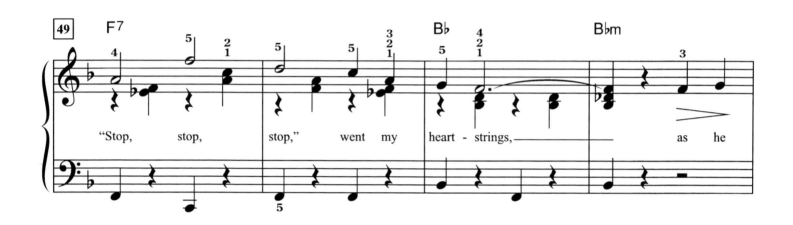

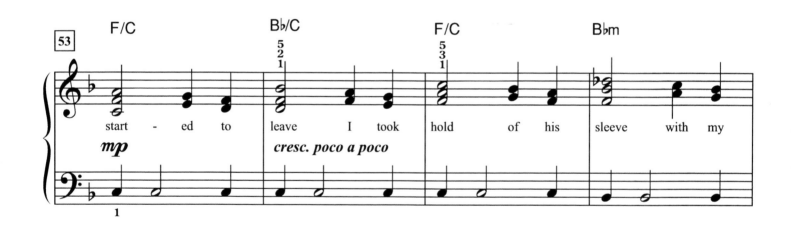

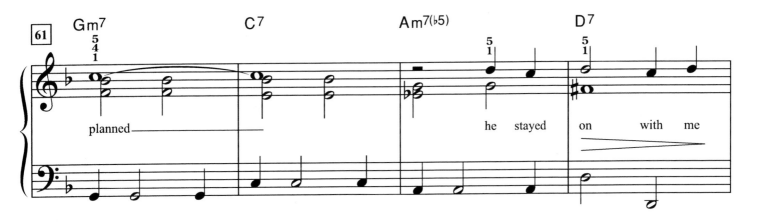

planned _____

he stayed on with me

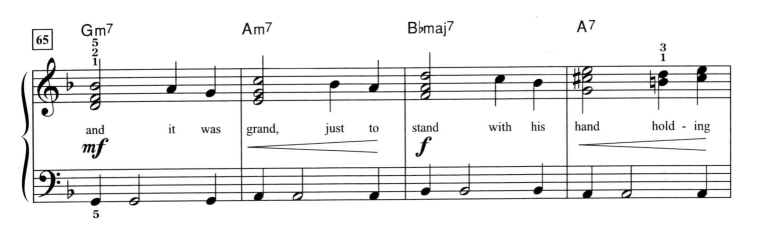

and it was grand, just to stand with his hand hold - ing

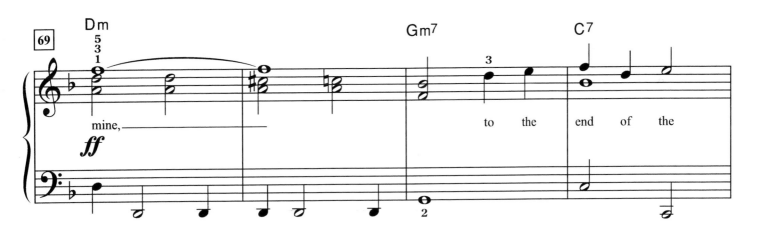

mine, _____

to the end of the

line. _____

TAKE ME OUT TO THE BALLGAME

In 1908, a subway sign that read "Baseball Today—Polo Grounds" inspired vaudeville star Jack Norworth to write what is now considered the unofficial anthem of baseball. He scribbled down the lyrics for the song on a scrap of paper which is now included in the permanent collection of baseball memorabilia at the National Baseball Hall of Fame. Tin Pan Alley composer and publisher Albert Von Tilzer co-wrote the music, and Norworth's wife, Nora Bayes, was the first of many vaudeville entertainers to perform the song. The song became so popular that the sales of Cracker Jack popcorn, which is mentioned in the lyrics, skyrocketed. Ironically, neither Norworth nor Von Tilzer attended a baseball game until decades after the song was written.

Words and Music by Jack Norworth and Albert Von Tilzer
Arranged by Dan Coates

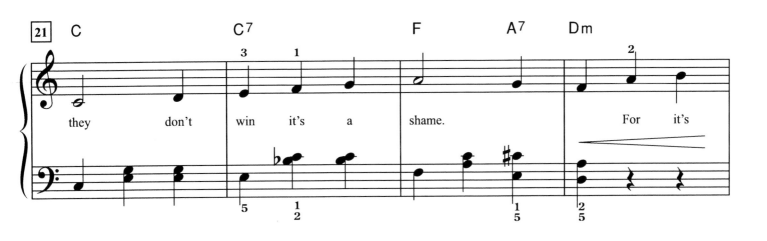

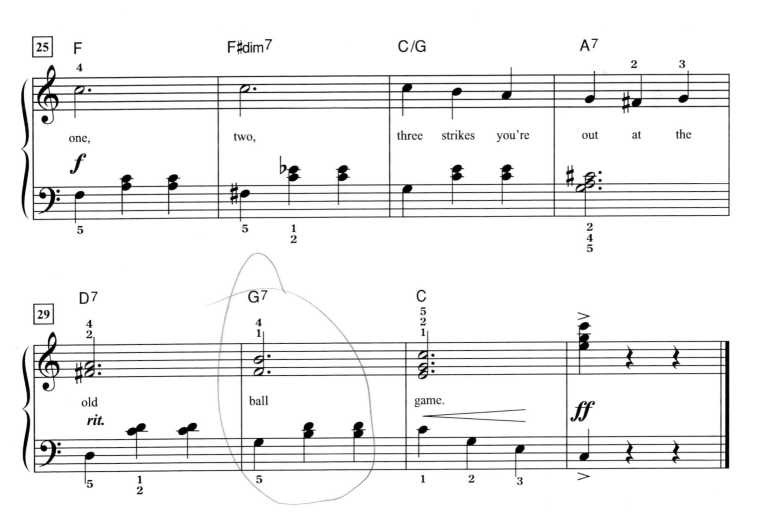

THE WAY YOU MAKE ME FEEL

"The Way You Make Me Feel" was the third consecutive #1 single from Michael Jackson's ninth album *Bad* (1987). Jackson famously performed the single at the 1988 Grammy Awards, as well as at his 30th anniversary concert in 2001 at Madison Square Garden with Britney Spears. The success of the album was supported by Jackson's 16-month, 123-concert worldwide *The Bad Tour*, the most successful tour of the '80s which grossed over $125 million.

Written and Composed by Michael Jackson
Arranged by Dan Coates

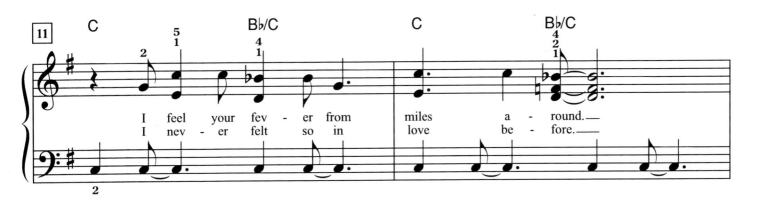

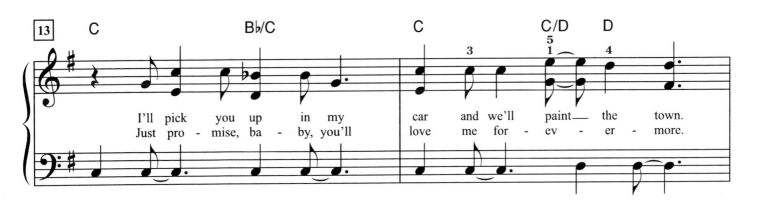

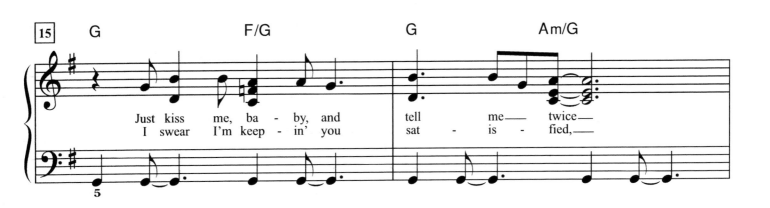

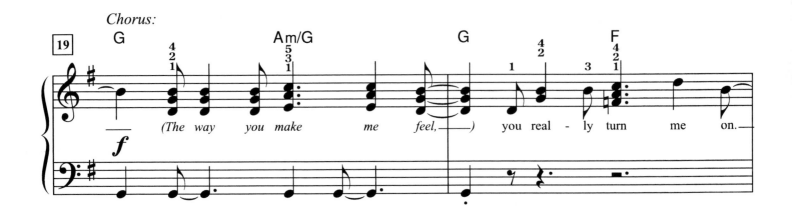

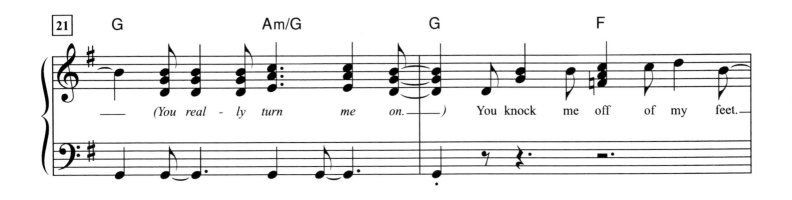

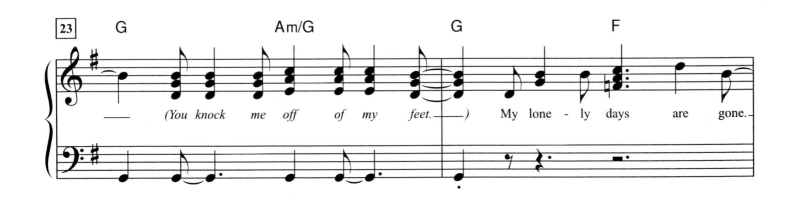

WHERE OR WHEN

"Where or When" was written for the 1937 Rodgers and Hart musical *Babes in Arms,* which featured many hit songs: "My Funny Valentine" (page 168), "The Lady Is a Tramp" (page 143), "Johnny One Note," and "I Wish I Were In Love Again." In 1939, the musical was made into a successful movie starring Mickey Rooney, who was nominated for an Oscar for his performance, and Judy Garland, who had just finished filming *The Wizard of Oz.*

Words by Lorenz Hart
Music by Richard Rodgers
Arranged by Dan Coates

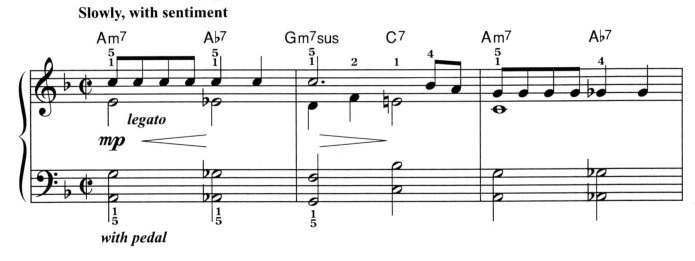

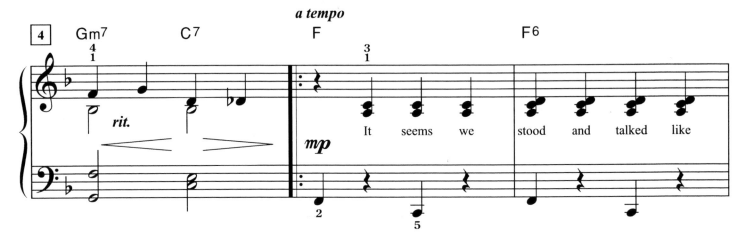

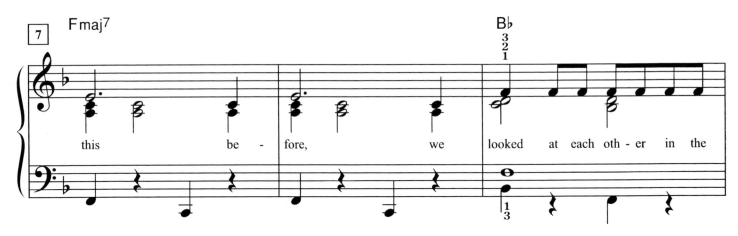

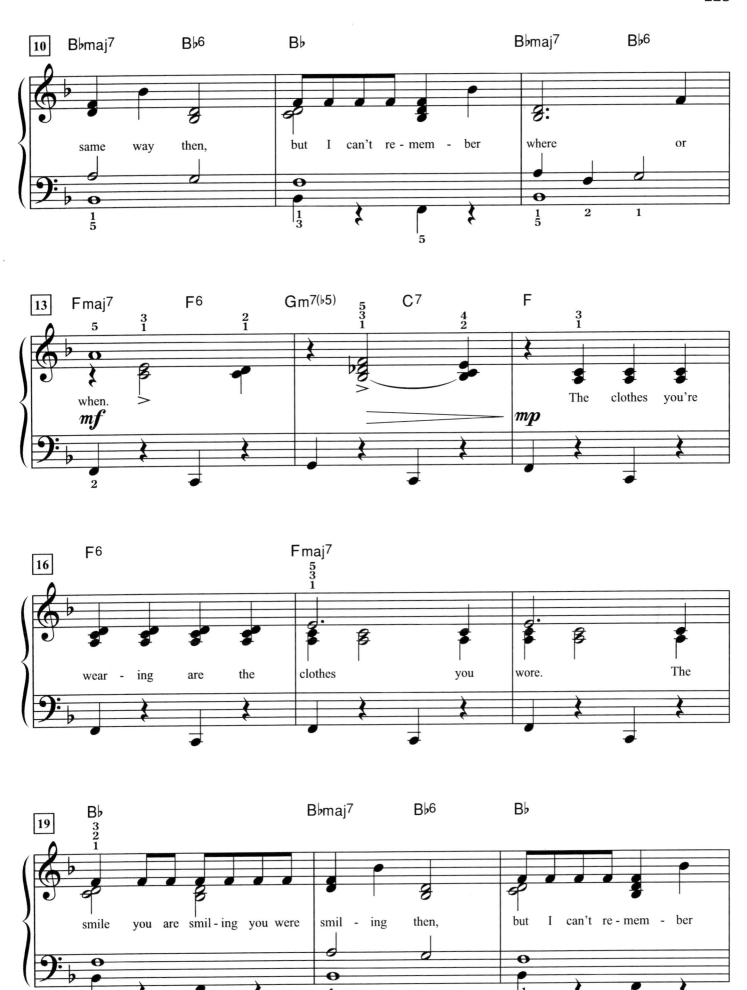

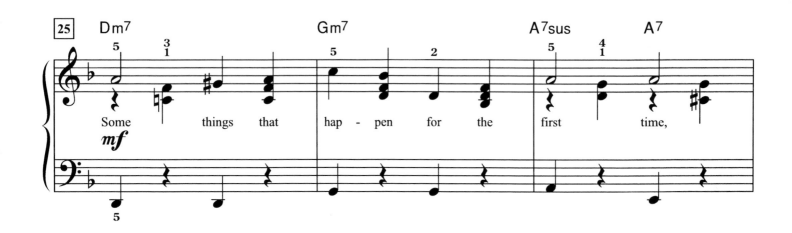

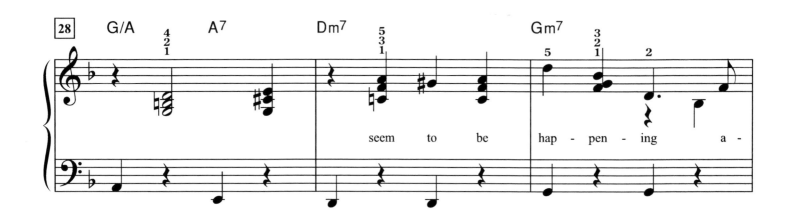

WE ARE THE WORLD

"We Are the World" was written in 1985 by Michael Jackson and Lionel Richie as a fundraising song to help provide relief for famine-stricken Ethiopia which had experienced unusual drought in 1984–85. USA for Africa (United Support of Artists for Africa) was a supergroup of musicians who recorded the song including Ray Charles, Bob Dylan, Michael Jackson, Billy Joel, Cyndi Lauper, Bette Midler, Willie Nelson, Lionel Richie, Smokey Robinson, Diana Ross, Paul Simon, Bruce Springsteen, Tina Turner, Dionne Warwick, Stevie Wonder, and many others. The song won four Grammy Awards and raised over $63 million.

Words and Music by
Michael Jackson and Lionel Richie
Arranged by Dan Coates

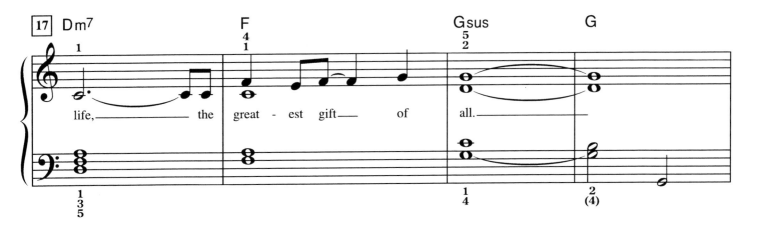

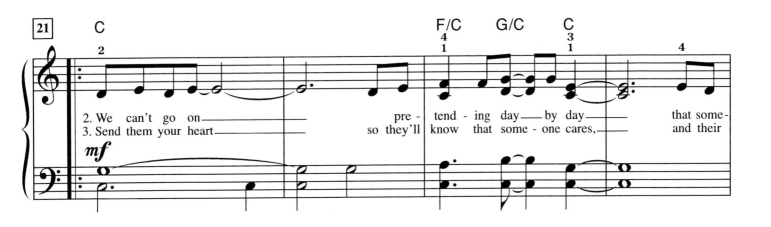

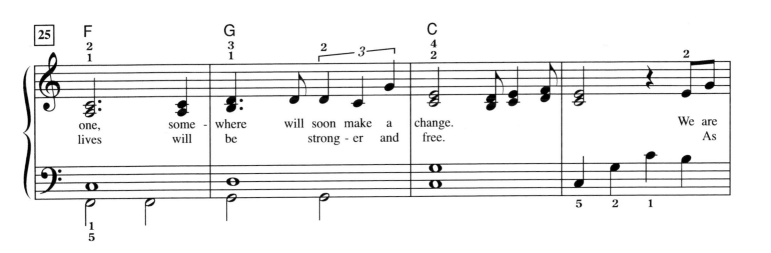

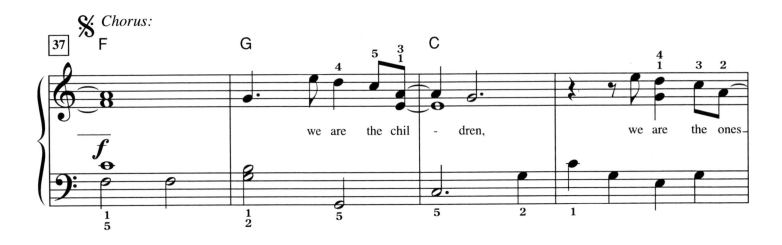

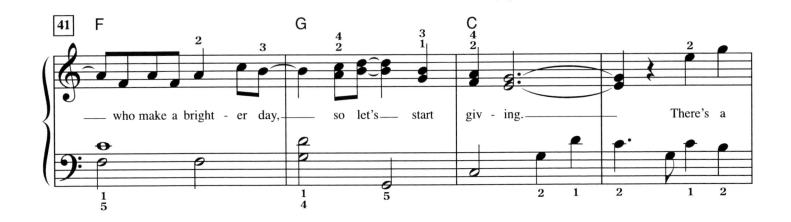

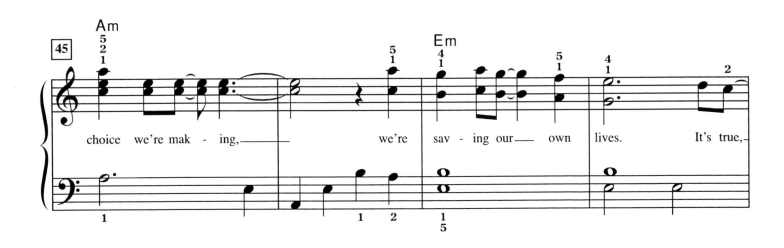

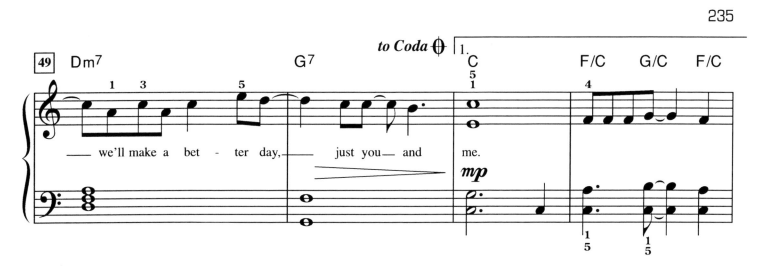

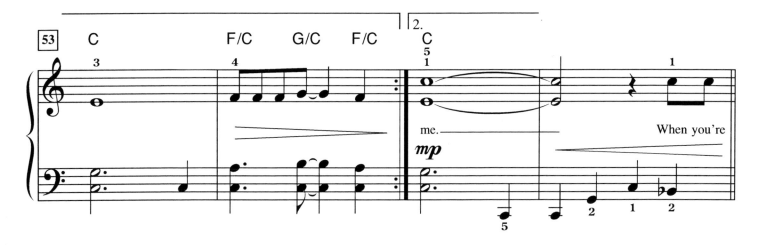

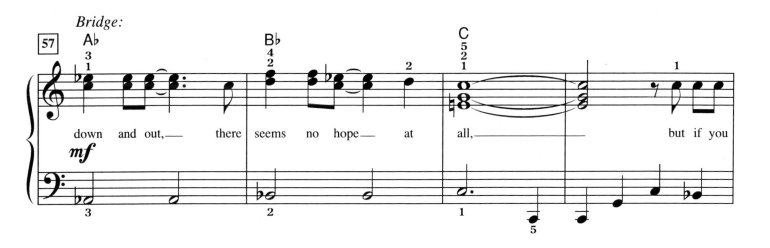

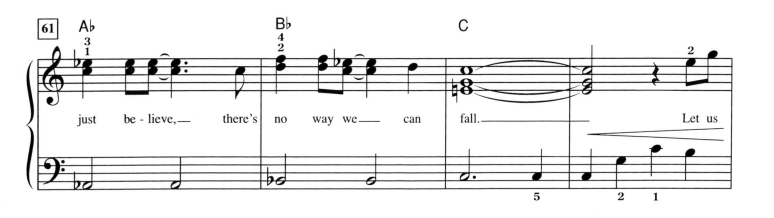

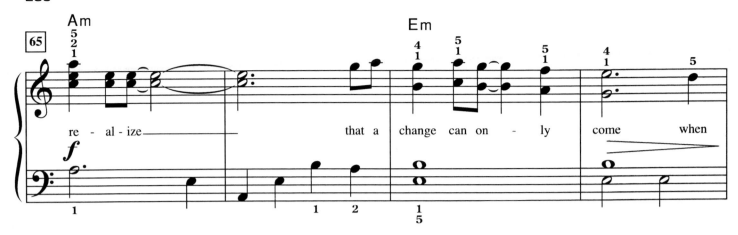

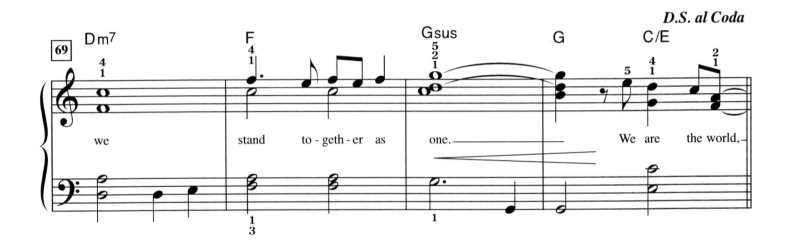

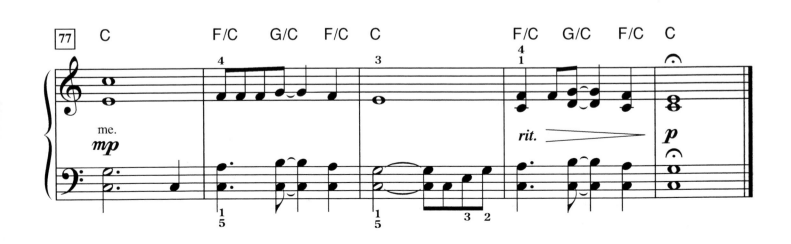

A WHOLE NEW WORLD
(from Walt Disney's *Aladdin*)

"A Whole New World" is the hit single from Walt Disney's animated feature *Aladdin* (1992). In the film it was sung by Brad (Caleb) Kane and Lea Salonga (the singing voices for Aladdin and Princess Jasmine) and during the closing credits by Peabo Bryson and Regina Belle. The ballad won the Academy Award for Best Original Song and became the only Disney song to hit #1 on the U.S. charts.

Words by Tim Rice
Music by Alan Menken
Arranged by Dan Coates

Chorus:

ride. A whole new world,_____ a new fan-

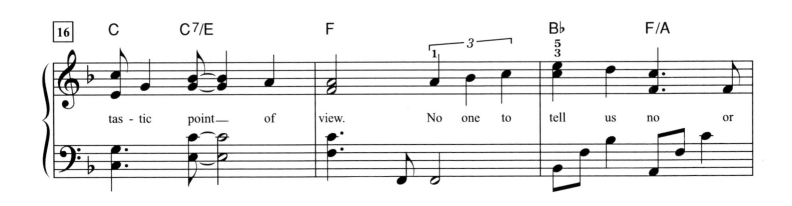

-tas - tic point___ of view. No one to tell us no or

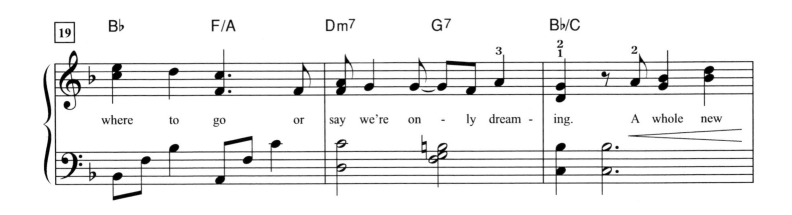

where to go or say we're on - ly dream - ing. A whole new

world,_____ a daz - zling place I nev - er

WIND BENEATH MY WINGS

"Wind Beneath My Wings" is known as Bette Midler's signature song. She recorded it in 1989 for the dramatic film *Beaches*, a movie in which she also starred. The single was a #1 hit and also won Record of the Year and Song of the Year at the 1990 Grammy Awards. A number of artists (Sheena Easton, Roger Whittaker, Gary Morris, Gladys Knight, and Lou Rawls) had recorded the song before Midler, yet none were as successful.

Words and Music by
Larry Henley and Jeff Silbar
Arranged by Dan Coates

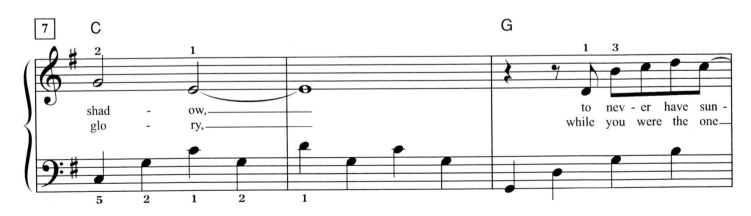

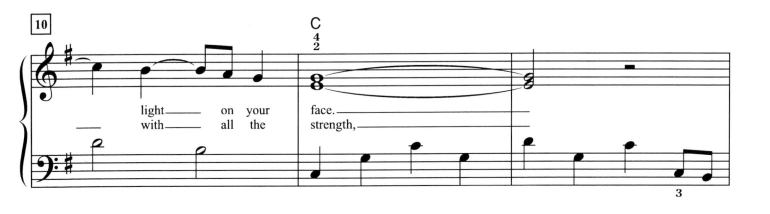

light_____ on your face._____
with_____ all the strength,_____

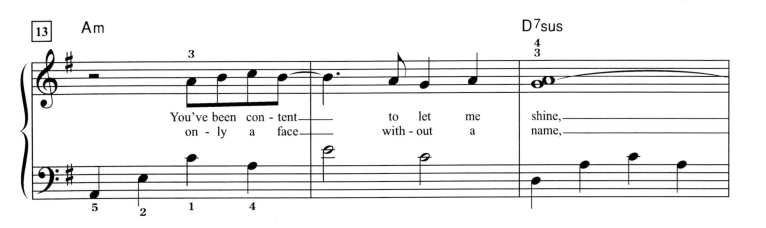

Am **D⁷sus**

You've been con - tent___ to let me shine,_____
on - ly a face___ with - out a name,_____

D **Am**

___ you al - ways walked___ a step be -
___ I nev - er once___ heard you com -

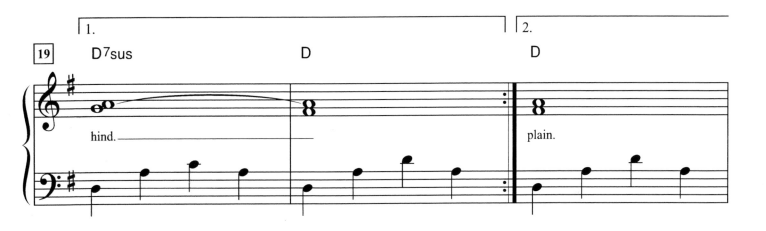

1. 2.

D⁷sus **D** **D**

hind._____
plain.

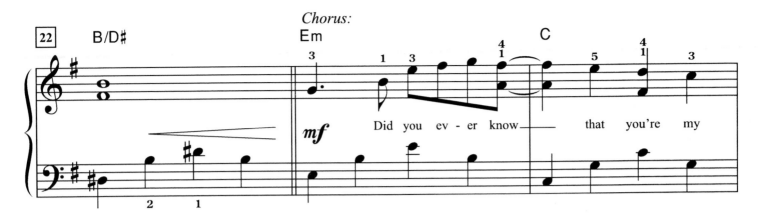

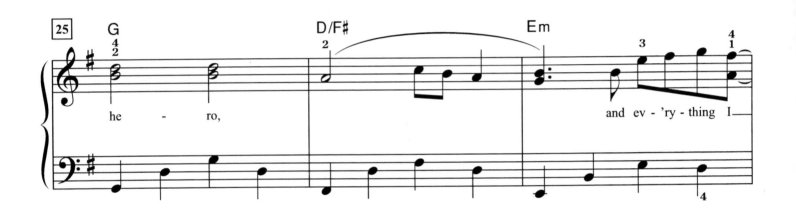

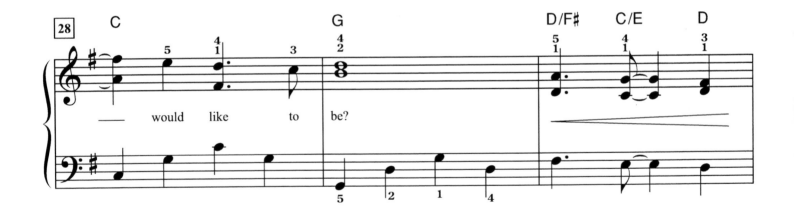

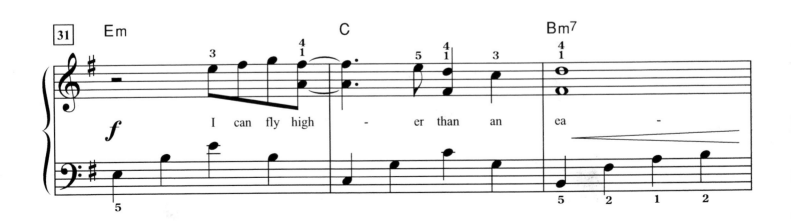

YANKEE DOODLE BOY

George M. Cohan's *Little Johnny Jones*, one of the first American musicals, opened on Broadway on November 7, 1904. The show, based on a true story, is about an American jockey who rides a horse named Yankee Doodle in the English Derby. "Yankee Doodle Boy" and "Give My Regards to Broadway" (page 74) are the two famous songs from the show. The former song was famously performed by James Cagney in the 1942 film *Yankee Doodle Dandy*, a biography about Cohan.

Word and Music by George M. Cohan
Arranged by Dan Coates

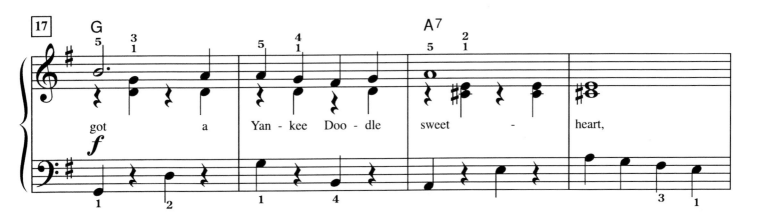

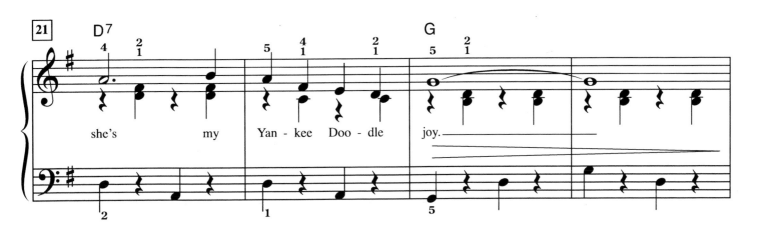

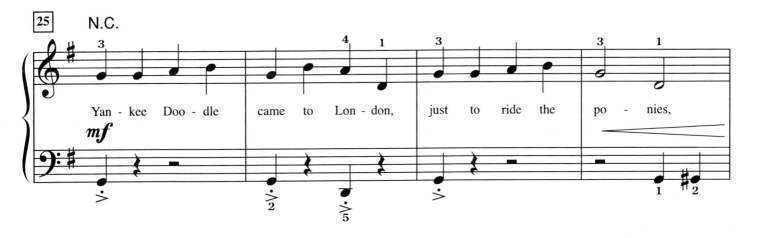

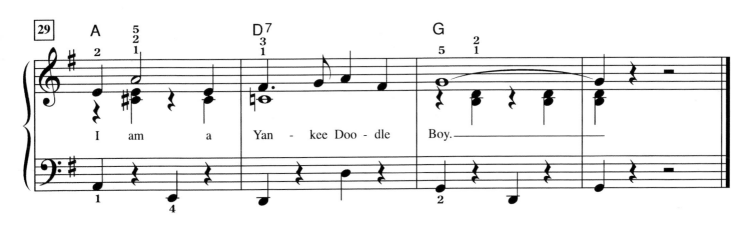

YOU LIGHT UP MY LIFE

"You Light Up My Life" was written for the 1977 romantic comedy/drama of the same name. Kasey Cisyk recorded the song for the movie, and Debby Boone, who is the daughter of '50s icon Pat Boone, recorded and released the song as a single. The single topped the Billboard Hot 100 for 10 weeks and became the most successful single of the '70s.

Words and Music by Joe Brooks
Arranged by Dan Coates

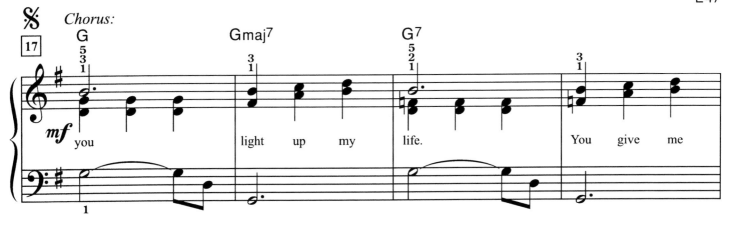

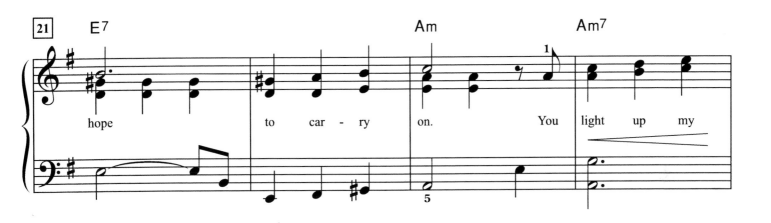

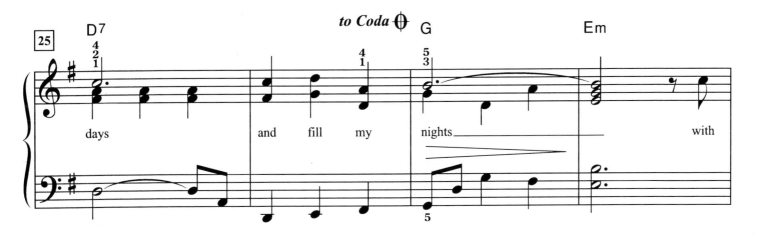

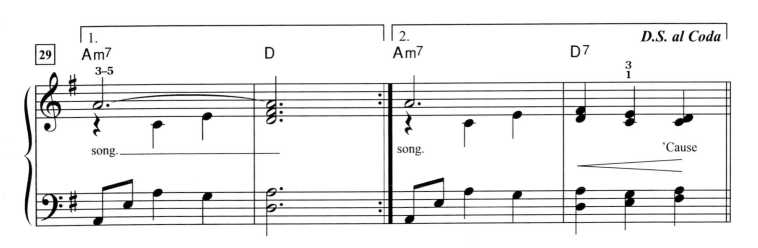

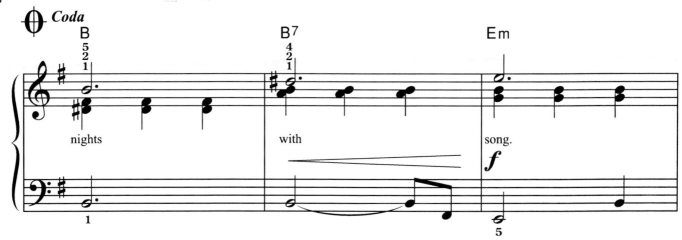

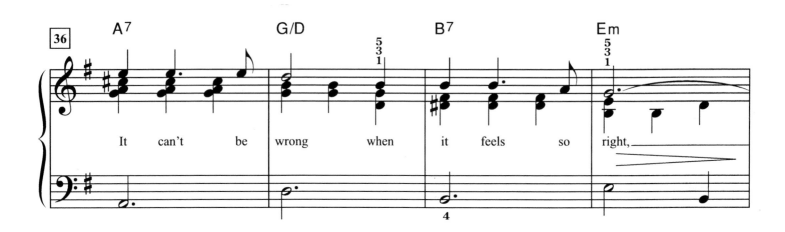

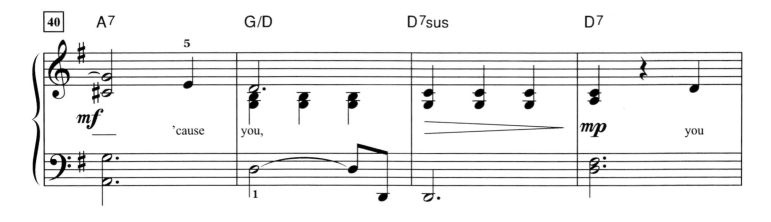

YOU RAISE ME UP

Josh Groban's version of "You Raise Me Up" was featured on his second album, 2003's *Closer*, and was nominated for a Grammy award. Though Groban is oft-associated with this single, it was written by Rolf Løvland and Brendan Graham of the New Age group Secret Garden and performed on their album *Once in a Red Moon* (released March, 2002) by Irish singer-songwriter Brian Kennedy.

Words and Music by Rolf Løvland and Brendan Graham
Arranged by Dan Coates

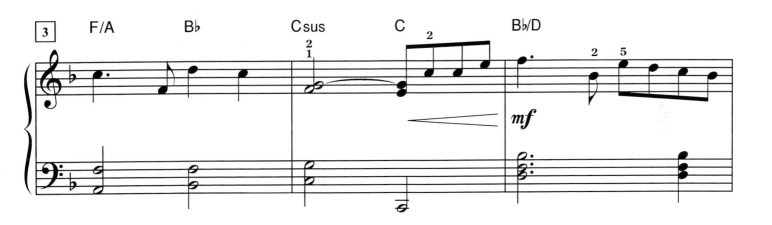

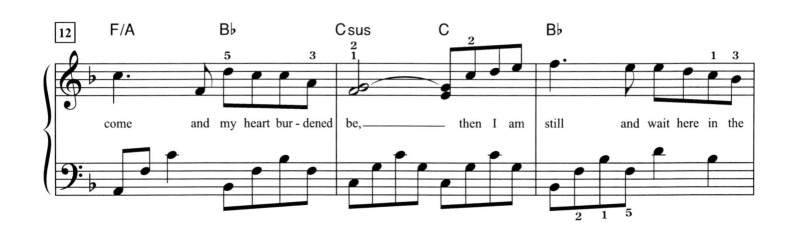

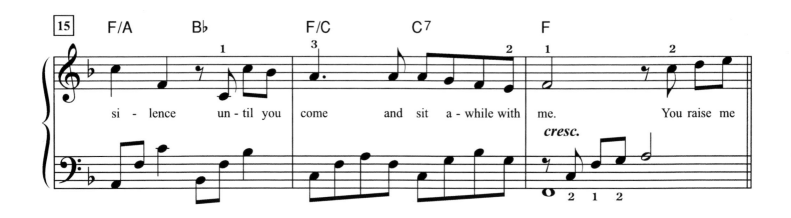

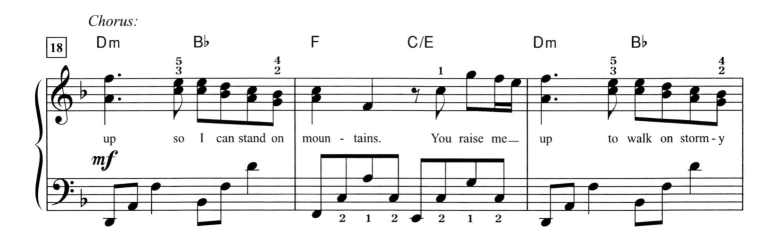

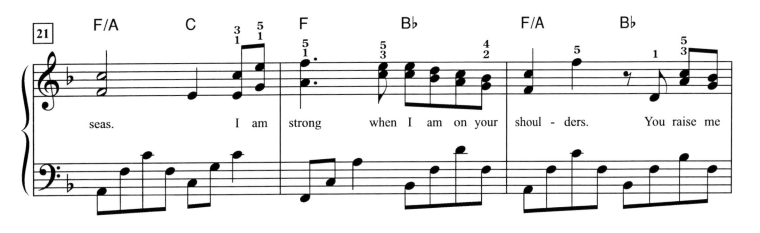

seas.　　I am　strong　when I am on your　shoul - ders.　　You raise me

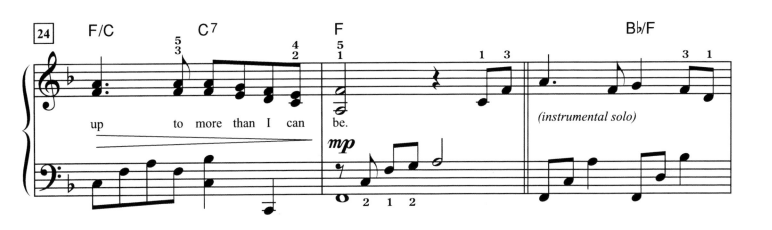

up　　to more than I can　be.　　*(instrumental solo)*

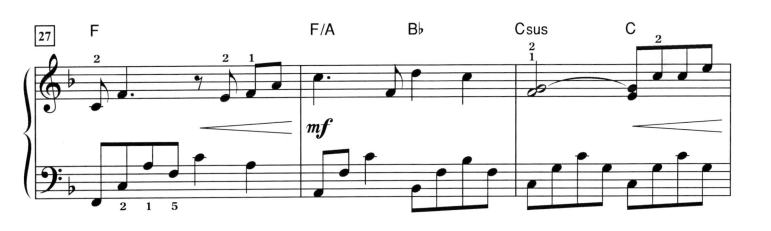

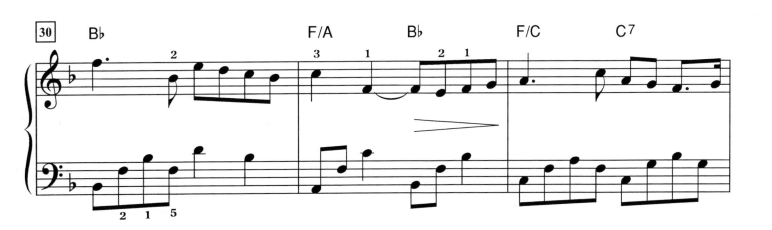

Chorus:

You raise me up so I can stand on moun - tains. You raise me—

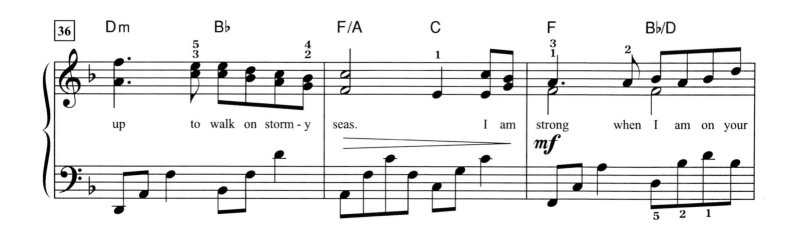

up to walk on storm - y seas. I am strong when I am on your

shoul - ders. You raise me up to more than I can be.

Chorus:

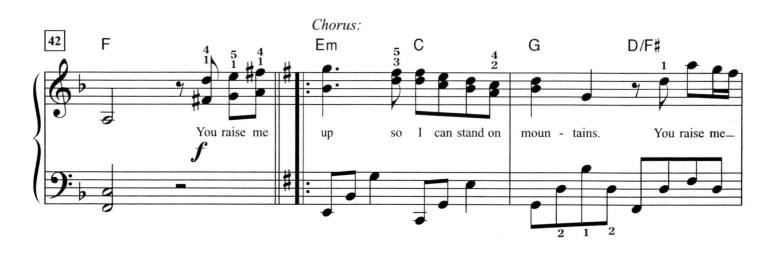

You raise me up so I can stand on moun - tains. You raise me—

ZIP-A-DEE-DOO-DAH

"Zip-A-Dee-Doo-Dah" is from the Walt Disney film *Song of the South* (1946), which was Disney's first film to feature both live-action and animated scenes. The movie was based on a cycle of stories by Joel Chandler Harris—a Georgia-born journalist of the post-Civil War era—and features Uncle Remus (a kindly, old, story-telling slave) and his fables of Br'er Rabbit (a likable trickster who perpetually finds himself in trouble). "Zip-A-Dee-Doo-Dah" was sung in the film by James Baskett, who played Uncle Remus. It won the 1947 Academy Award for Best Song and has become a Disney classic. Additionally, *Song of the South* is the inspiration for Splash Mountain, the famous water ride at Disney theme parks.

Words by Ray Gilbert
Music by Allie Wrubel
Arranged by Dan Coates

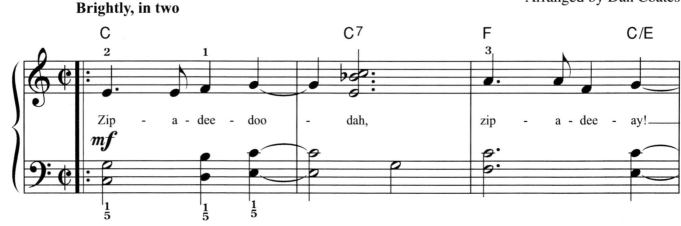

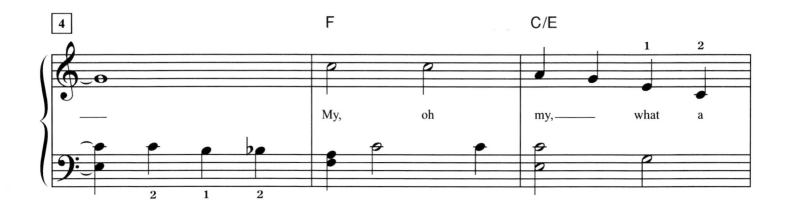

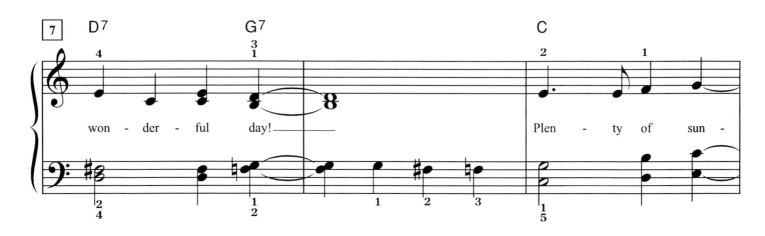

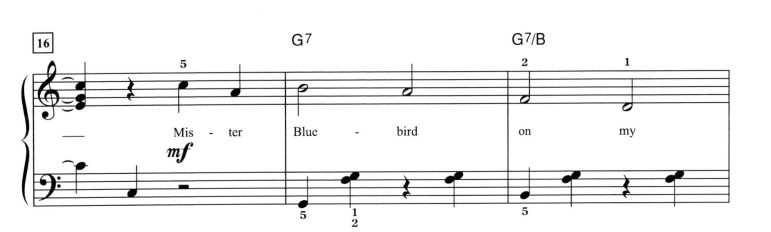

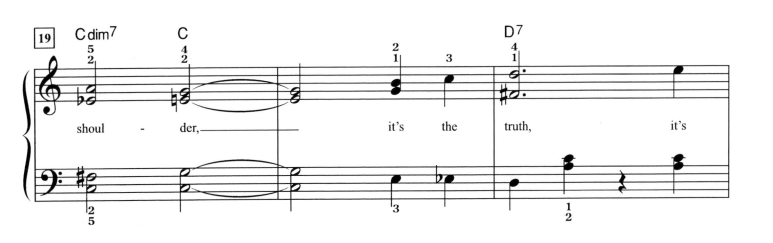

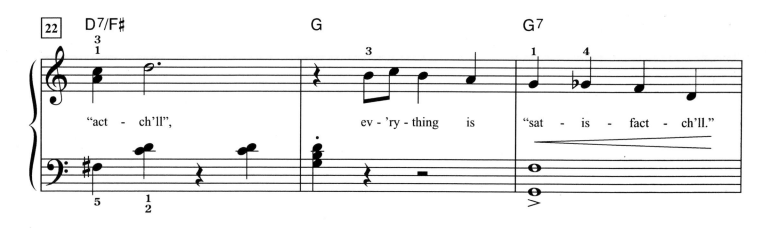

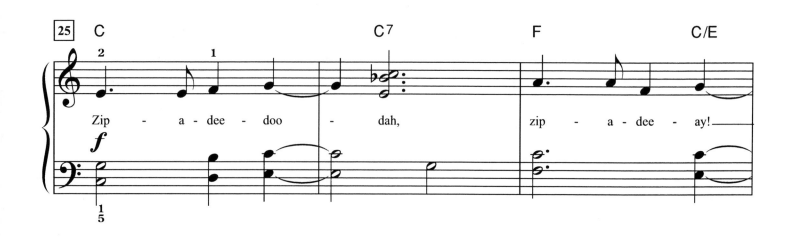

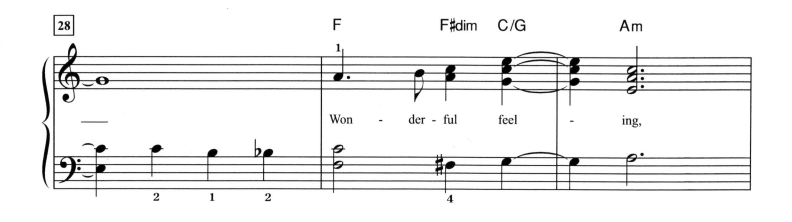

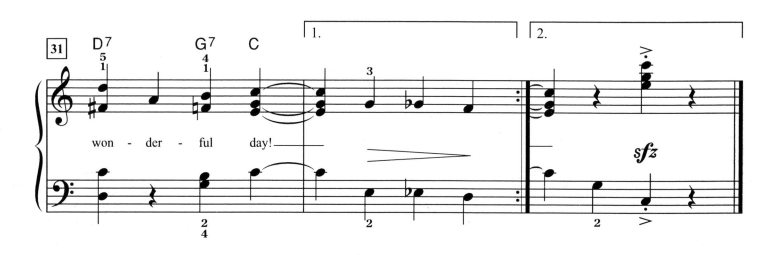